THE
MANIFESTOS AND ESSAYS

THE
MANIFESTOS AND ESSAYS

Richard Foreman

THEATRE COMMUNICATIONS GROUP
NEW YORK
2013

The Manifestos and Essays is published by Theatre Communications Group, Inc., 520 Eighth Avenue, 24th Floor, New York, NY 10018-4156.

The publication of *The Manifestos and Essays* by Richard Foreman is made possible in part by the New York State Council on the Arts with the support of Governor Andrew Cuomo and the New York State Legislature.

TCG books are exclusively distributed to the book trade by Consortium Book Sales and Distribution.

LIBRARY OF CONGRESS CATALOGING-IN-PUBLICATION DATA

Foreman, Richard, 1937–
[Essays. Selections]
The manifestos and essays / Richard Foreman.—First edition.
pages cm
Includes bibliographical references.
ISBN 978-1-55936-398-3 (trade paper)
ISBN 978-1-55936-652-6 (ebook)
I. Title.
PS3556.O7225A6 2013
814'.54—dc23
2013002064
Cover and book design and composition by Lisa Govan
Cover photograph by Anne Nordmann

First Edition, October 2013

CONTENTS

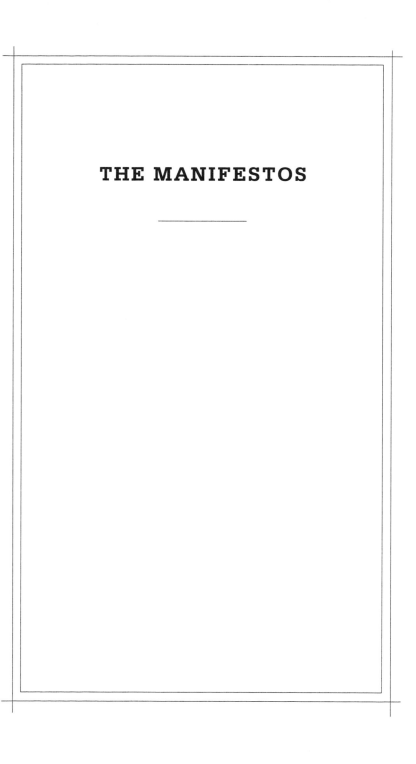

THE MANIFESTOS

ONTOLOGICAL-HYSTERIC MANIFESTO I

(APRIL, 1972)

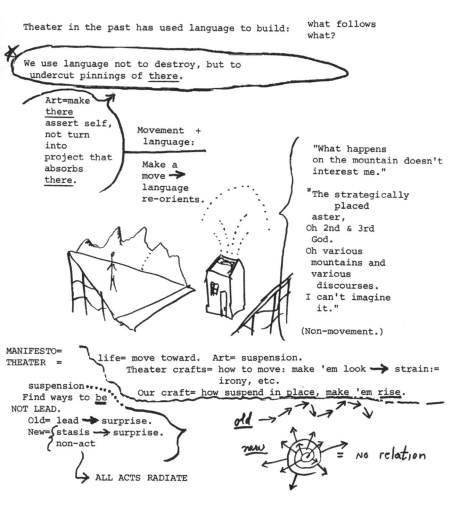

Theater in the past has used language to build: what follows what?

We use language not to destroy, but to undercut pinnings of <u>there</u>.

Art=make <u>there</u> assert self, not turn into project that absorbs <u>there</u>.

Movement + language:

Make a move → language re-orients.

"What happens on the mountain doesn't interest me."

"The strategically placed aster, Oh 2nd & 3rd God. Oh various mountains and various discourses. I can't imagine it."

(Non-movement.)

MANIFESTO= THEATER =

life= move toward. Art= suspension.

Theater crafts= how to move: make 'em look → strain:= irony, etc.

suspension

Find ways to be NOT LEAD.

Our craft= <u>how suspend in place, make 'em rise</u>.

Old= lead → surprise.

New=⎰stasis → surprise.
　　⎱non-act

old →

new

= No relation

ALL ACTS RADIATE

THEATER

The stage. Destroy it carefully, not with
effort but with delicate maneuvers.

Why? Heavy destruction vs. light destruction.
What distorts is excellent.
What distorts with its weight.

Distortions: 1) logic -- as in realism, which we reject
because the mind already "knows" the next move and so
is not alive to that next move.
        2) chance & accident & the arbitrary -- which
we reject because within too short a time each choice so
determined becomes equally predictable as "item produced
by chance, accident, etc."
        3) the new possibility (what distorts with
its weight) -- a subtle insertion between logic and
accident, which keeps the mind alive as it evades over-
quick integration into the mental system. CHOOSE THIS ALWAYS!

        The field of the play is distorted by the
objects within the play, so that each object distorts each
other object and the mental pre-set is excluded.

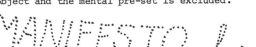

Problem of art-- how
to make people watch
the right thing while
it's going on...   SO ──────────>

Not watch changing
relations:
But watch what
doesn't   change   in
midst of it.....

"Language
subjects us
to orien-
tation
massage." --
Peckham:
that's
all.

Art: not concerned with essence
But with THING
used in such a way
that it vanishes
& what is
left is suspension:
In life.──>.thing is tool --we get
somewhere.
In art.<─> never get there
Suspended.
Why? Create a ZONE
in which placed
things (head) luminate!

1967-- Suddenly the theater seems ridiculous in all its
manifestations and continues to do so in 1971. I.e.,
Peter Brook staged Midsummer Night's Dream. The actors
enter onstage and immediately, the absurdity-- both
in the orchestrated speech and activity-- as Stella,
Judd, et al. realized several years ago...one must reject
composition in favor of shape (or something else)...
Why? Because the resonance must be between the head
and the object. The resonance between the elements
of the object is now a DEAD THING.

1971--Lenox, summer. I sit, at sunrise, and stare out
into the trees, listening to the birds-- i.e. 100
invisible birds in counterpoint. My head, savoring
that interweaving of themes, performs in a good way--
performs in the way that heretofore I have felt art
should make it perform. But suddenly (drama!)
that often-before entertained notion crystallizes in
my head in such a way that a chapter ends, the book
closes, and I have no more interest (no more risk,
no more "unknown") in such an art based on counterpoint & relationship. What can replace it? Don't
know.... The painters have discovered "shape." What
can the theater discover?

I.E.

Only one theatrical problem exists now: How to
create a stage performance in which the spectator
experiences the danger of art not as involvement or
risk or excitement, not as something that reaches out
to vulnerable areas of his person,
        but rather
the danger as a possible <u>decision</u> he (spectator) may
make upon the occasion of confronting the work of art.
The work of art as a <u>contest</u> between object (or
prócess) and viewer. Old notions of drama (up thru
Grotowski-Brook-Chaikin)= the danger of circumstance
turning in such a way that we are "trapped" in an
emotional commitment of one sort or another.
The new ontological mode of theater (within which
hysteria lies as a seed/spark which forces the
unseeable to cast shadows) --
The ontological-hysteric theater: the danger that
arises when one chooses to climb a mountain and-- half-
way up-- wishes one hadn't.

> Art till now= appealingness: Making an object
> that we fall in love with. Make the obsessional
> object.

        NOT ART/No more art, naturally. Yet the aesthetic
thrill. The point is, of course, that "art" no longer
provides (provokes?) the aesthetic thrill. In a world
of scarcity (now psychically superceded if not yet
practically) the one was against the other.
Conflict at root of drama. OK. It's all so simple,
really. Now-- art can't be based in conflict. Old art
aroused, empathized with that, made our inner nature
vibrate to that in such a way that it was "profound."
The grounds of conflict are now seen as...not between
entities, but within the single unitary occasion which
could exist-- could not exist. That oscillation
replacing "conflict."

where oscillates the conflict ?
conflict o —→ ← o
conflict ← o —→
. . . . ?

But there is no center, the conflict is between the idea
of a center and the idea of a field. (The idea of a
center= old-fashioned "being"; the idea of a field=
old-fashioned "not-being.")

A FIELD BY ITS NATURE CONTAINS ONLY HARMONY.
In our attempt to hold together a center, we mistakenly
    view the field perhaps as one in which particles,
    etc., form a kind of conflict situation. But:
Not true.
Conflict there, as elsewhere, an illusion. (Absence
    of conflict doesn't mean absence of dynamics.
    Conflict BLOCKS dynamics.
Ecstasy = all forces operate at once to produce STASIS!
          (Replace conflict-- push and pull of selected
           forces-- with total action of all forces.
           That is stasis, that is ecstasy.)

Wittgenstein:
If mean= intend. Anything is intended.
Any intend.
Use anything, to mean anything: but, the system must
    have a rigor.
Mean something by a movement·of the hand-- was it the
    movement that he meant?

To express something which can only be expressed by this
    movement.

To read off the "said" from the face of the thought?
No-- our theater is making harmony. Singing counterpoint
    in language-- swimming in language in a way
    appropriate to the ongoing internal (mental) activity..

So : language systems:
        THUD!
        (Start out speaking in own terms,
        system created in terms of play
        by using own concerns!)

$$\left(\begin{array}{l} \text{think of swimming, think of singing,} \\ \quad \text{think of the picnic, think of the grass} \\ \qquad \text{glass} \\ \qquad \text{glass} \\ \qquad \text{glass.} \\ \text{(Has a system begun to be created?)} \end{array} \right)$$

Now:

Acting against materials (the table, the floor, the other actor's body) is establishing this new language that doesn't <u>read</u> but "illustrates." (I.e., thinking against things.)　　　　Pick proper interference. Like new <u>motor</u>.

$$\underline{MOTOR} + \Big/ \frac{\underline{slight \; shifts}}{\underline{stuckness}\,?} \longrightarrow glue:$$

ALWAYS NOTATE YOUR EXACT SITUATION AND PROCESS WHEN <u>WRITING!</u>

TAKE TWO RULES CONTRADICTORY IN NATURE.　FOLLOWING BOTH MEANS SUCCESS.

In 1968, the theater became hopeless.　I suppose the immediate revulsion is always against the artificiality or something related to that, although artificiality itself is noble enough-- being the HUMAN contribution which, if properly posited, lifts the moment...turns nature herself into a construct of delight.

Ah-- that is the point is it not?　To make a construct, which must be the motive behind all art effort.　So where does the theater's artificiality turn sour?　At what point does the "construct" give way to the lie, to the exaggeration?　That may be the point: to isolate the difference between exaggeration and invention.　Whereas exaggeration destroys balance, and invention is constantly replacing the center of harmony, shifting it

slightly in such a way that the shift, the moment of shift,
the act of the shift, becomes-- if experienced as the
specific OCCURRING EVENT that it is-- an occasion for
testing oneself, as climbing a mountain is a test of the
body.
Art, of course, tests the soul, tests the psyche. That
is to say-- purely a matter of vibrations. Now, where
do these vibrations vibrate? What fluid is it in which
the resonating wave patterns are established?

Well, folks-- ! The vibrations are in the head, of course.
And they are most certainly produced by the
(demonstratable) scanning mechanism of the brain. And
the universe-- which exists to us as a direct "production"
of that scanning and in-the-instant-rescanning, must
enter into a new relationship to the art work. No longer
the relation between a changing world (events march on)
and a posited ego which VIEWS events and in so doing
EXTRACTS art from the flux of the world-- while in that
EXTRACTION lies the terror that manifests itself as
"conflict and expression" in drama.....but a (new)
relationship in which the world is essentially a
repeating mechanism (which it is on both its building
block level and its higher cyclic levels) and the
scanning mechanism superimposed on the repeating mechanism
slowly builds an edifice. (The way nature and history
build.)

Two DIFFERENT kinds of edifice are built, however. One of
them is called "life" (in the private sense of "I have
lived a life") ...and the other shall be called art,
though this "art" is clearly something different from what
has been called art up to this point.

For this new "art"-- perhaps we should not think of it as
an edifice but as an accretion, as deposited sludge--
this new art is not EXTRACTED from the flux of life, and is
therefore in no sense a mirror or representation-- but a
parallel phenomenon to life itself. The scanning
mechanism produces the lived experience when it is
passive. I.e., the input rhythms are dominant; and the
scanning mechanism produces art when it is the ACTIVE
element, when its rhythms dominate the scanned object.
(The actual "making" of the art object then becomes
essentially a matter of notation.)

So hopefully, we end up with a new art that serves two
essential, related functions:
1) Evidence: useful as example to others, of the harmony
that results from an awareness and conscious employment
of our mechanism which is our "self" in its properly
industrious way upon the world (that flux of "everything
that is the case").
Evidence....to give courage to ourself and others to be
alive from moment to moment, which means to accept both
flux (presentation and representation to consciousness
as reality) and an INTERSECTING process--scanning--which
is the perpetual constituting and reconstituting of the
self.   The new work of art-as-evidence leaves a <u>tracing</u>
<u>in matter</u> of this intersecting, and encourages a
courageous "tuning" of the old self to the new awareness.

2) ORDEAL. The artistic experience <u>must</u> be an ordeal to
be undergone. The rhythms <u>must</u> be in a certain way
difficult and uncongenial. Uncongenial elements are then
redeemed by a clarity in the moment-to-moment, smallest
unit of progression. After all-- clarity is relatively
easy (at least the "feeling" of clarity) in terms of
large structures because simplification can always be
wrought on a large structure (simplification often being
the bastardization of clarity).
But CLARITY is so difficult in the smallest steps from
one moment to the next, because on the miniscule level,
clarity is muddled either by the "logic" of progression
(which is really a form of sleepwalking) or by the
predictability of the opposite choice-- the surreal-
absurdist choice of the arbitrary & accidental &
haphazard step.
Of course
 ORDEAL
is the only experience that remains. And clarity is the
mode in which the ordeal becomes ecstatic.

Art is not beauty of
description or depth of
emotion, it is making a
machine, not to do some-
thing to audience, but that
makes itself run on new
fuel. Can this machine
run? Most machines (art)
run on audience fuel--
(Man's piggish desire to
be at the center, to be
made to feel there is
"caringness" built into
the world: old art
manipulates that, tries to
get a response: fuel is
DESIRE in that case.
 FIND FUEL OTHER THAN
 DESIRE! Nervous energy?
 Basic hum of life?
 Vibration?) (Desire
 kills vibration, gets
 too crude)

WE MAKE A PERPETUAL
MOTION MACHINE. (The
closer to that ideal the
better. Run on less and
less fuel...that's the
goal of the new art
machine.)

I   REPEAT !

I want to be seized by the elusive, unexpected aliveness
of the moment.
Surprise at the center: not the surprise of the least-
expected.....because that (least-expected) is a reaction
that "places" it and makes it no longer elusive. But
surprised by
a freshness
of moment that eludes
                constantly refreshes. You go toward it
and can't seize it? You don't go toward it...........

Art to me=
energy of wantin
to know (alert)
without desire t
move off the
center, off the
energy itself to
the object. Be
happy NOT knowin
in condition of
wanting to know.
Be joyous in tha
tension.

        Most art is
        created by
        people trying to
        make their idea,
        emotion, thing-
        imagined, be-there
        more. They re-
        inforce. I want
        my imagined to be an

Write by thinkin
against the
material. Since
you don't want
to convince self
of your vision,
etc.-- but to le
it be informed b
the disintegrati
now-moment.

occasion wherein the not-imagined-by-me can be there.
My work= to deny my assertion (imagined) is true (is
there).
    by letting moment disintegrate it, as no assertion
really true in the face of the elusive now, the real
moment, which in its bottomlessness turns what it holds
into the bottomless anti-matter of what is itself in
the rigidity and deadness of before and after.

Subject of theater-- vanity: in all: nothing real
or of any great matter, including <u>that</u> fact: So it is
ALL THEATER.

1) Used to be--   like a staggered race
Relations (beauty)
Now that's a cliché.
So-- no relations:
But shape?   relates to head

Head: keep dealing with throb in head.

2) Undercut
Set up irritant
against line of the scene.
(Bright lights?)
intersect with other realm.

Don't sustain anything

1) Erotic angel: --a shape

Subject: THE EFFORT OF PUTTING WHATEVER ARISES TOGETHER
That <u>EFFORT</u>.

Subject: Make everything dumb enough to allow what is
really happening to happen.

MAN occurs in   gap: joint...

Joints
one thing = other:

"a new cadence means a new idea."

only: *get*

rhythm of the mind as something that acts
vis-a-vis entering dots: which leave <u>traces</u> that other
dots bounce off. So mind is input folded over imput.
GET THAT!

Manifesto !

*In which
everything
achieves a
final form.*

BEN: (That writing) says "I gave up writing plays
three years ago." (<u>Pause</u>.) The fat lamp descends.
That is not written but imagined. (<u>Pause</u>.)
Come into the writer's workshop.

<u>A second lamp down, hanging over the first. A hum.</u>

Get that second lamp outa here.

LEGEND: "WHY?"

BEN: Nobody has a right to ask me questions who doesn't
      show himself.

Crew comes and closes curtains on screen on which title
is projected.

      Why.

Thud, pause.

      The minute I formed that word carefully it was
      an imitation.

The curtain reopens by itself. A slide of an ancient
auto is projected on the screen. Pause. Then the same
picture is projected on the table-top.

  VOICE: One picture must not be allowed to view the
          other picture.

Music begins. A sign comes down--"Cousins in
photography." The music stops. Ben has exited. He
returns with a rope, throws it over the screen, with a
hook on the end of the rope, and starts to pull.

BEN: Oh well. (Pause.) Make something.
ALL: Can you describe it, Ben?

ONTOLOGICAL-HYSTERIC MANIFESTO II

(JULY, 1974)

One always begins with the desire to write a certain kind of sentence (to put on stage a certain "kind" of gesture. That "kind" then turns out to be about that-which-becomes-your-content).

The key, however, is in this sentence (gesture) cell. Most people don't see the cell, are perceptually unable to see small enough (ephemeralization). Because their LIFE training is that to "see small" means to enter the realm where contradictions are seen to be at the root of reality—and that disturbing realization they would avoid at all costs.

The desire to write a certain kind of sentence (gesture) is akin to the desire to live—be—have the world be in a certain kind of way. (Art as a solution to what is—Musil. Through style, through smallest possible units. Bricks determine one style of architecture, stone another, etc.)

> *(A solution to the problem of what is*
> *doesn't imply a utopian vision—how*
> *to fix the world—but how to BE*
> *so that*
> *One can respond to the world-as-it-is*
> *instead of*
> *responding to a dream world, an inherited*

> *world in which institutions and training*
> *hypnotize us so we see THEIR version of*
> *reality.)*

To UNDERSTAND the work is to understand the cell, and the possibilities and implications latent in the cell, just as the possibilities and
implications latent in atom and molecular biology lead to a view of life
and universe—the end in both cases being a patterned energy system.

Reach the pre-conscious: remove the personality.

Make the acts of the play not be "aimed" acts but isomorphic with the
pre-conscious and its richness. In other words, acts that on each occasion evoke the *source*—rather than acts (as in daily life) which pick an
object of desire and, in isolating that object from the whole constituting
field, are the very means by which we cut ourselves off from the source.

Detach (abstract) acts from sensuousness (desire-aim) ground.
Make acts be a form of wisdom. (Thinking)
(Speaking)

> We are usually told that art should root itself in the concrete. That
> means—object-making, image-making, hypnotizing man with idols
> (beautiful things, stirring emotions, seductive personalities).
> No, man's task is to respect the imbalance in himself (Ortega)
> between nature (his outside—the concrete) and spirit (his inside—
> abstraction and dream). The concrete is what RESISTS man—so
> that he finds himself in that resistance. The TRUTH of man is that
> moment by moment resistance of the concrete—the concrete which
> RESISTS the inner project of abstraction, ephemeralization. FOR
> art to root itself in the concrete is to make the spectator believe
> for a while that he is either animal (who is that being who totally
> adjusts to nature—if it does not, it simply ceases to exist) or God
> (who is totally isomorphic with abstraction, dream, idea—for whom
> the wish IS the reality without the resistance of nature interfering).

Only art ROOTED in the abstract smallest unit of sentence or gesture as a KIND of projection of inner, which then stumbles over "nature"
(outer), reflects the truth of man's condition. Classical Realism, classical

Romanticism (which includes, of course, Surrealism, Expressionism, etc.) puts man to sleep—returning him to animal nature or deluding him that his dreams are objectively real.

If a work of art has a MESSAGE it means it is putting the spectator to sleep. The minute man "knows," he sleeps (Shestov). Because he loses touch with that IMBALANCE which he most deeply is. Art must keep man consciously rooted in that imbalance—and that can only be done if no conclusions are drawn (implied—as in the MESSAGE or RESOLUTION)—but rather, the spectator is moment by moment exposed to the true process of a certain kind of sentence-gesture (man's inner quest for style, for a way of being-in-the-world) as it encounters the resistance of the real-object (nature).

So the work of art is ROOTED and PROCEEDS from the abstract (spiritual, inner) and uses the ABSTRACT as content—which content finds it HARD TO EXIST in the world of the object (nature) and that is the grand music which the work captures because that is TO-BE-MAN.

That's what it means to say "images alone don't make anything new happen." The concrete image is an idol; empathy with an interesting character is the creation of an IDOL. We have an obligation to return the spectator to his own proper human space; oscillating back and forth between the frontiers of animal and God.

No "development" is possible. It's false when it occurs in a work of today. It's a reversion to primitivism. (Which is, of course, what people want, what we all want—to sink back into nature and sleep. To sink back into the mother—to end "stress.") Development is the negation of stress, or rather the avoidance of stress. To return to the one human point—that imbalance between inner and outer—is to sit on the one true stress-point that is never resolved—just as the STRESS which is being-a-human is never resolved (unless one finally does opt for animal or God), DEVELOPMENT in a work of art is a giving-up, a moving-off that stress point into animalism or spiritualism. In both cases—dreaming, wish fulfillment, going to sleep.

When we say "development," perhaps to be more exact, we should notice that development generally means the development of each item from the preceding item of a series—and it is this which is false. ANOTHER sort of development exists—details proceeding from an idea of the whole living-field.

The "impossible," "false" developmental procedure in current art would be step A proceeding from step B—such development can be nothing but hypnotism and lie.

The only development possible which leaves us free to be awake and be human in our watching is one in which each detail proceeds from a continual referral back to the constituting process of consciousness colliding with world—the process that makes things for us "be."

Bad art, Kitsch, develops detail from preceding detail. That is, the "previous" fact is an object, the "response" to (development from) that object is another object, and so on.

Creating a network of objects.
Idols.
Imprisonment.

We IGNORE the preceding fact or act—so it is allowed to VANISH as it should when its moment of being-there has passed—so the NEW can arise, moment by moment.

If each moment is new, if we die to each moment as it arises, we are alive. Development (sequential) is death. Is objectification. Is idol-making. Drama as it has been focuses on conflict between formed entities. (Idols. Dead things. Hamlet as a dead thing—to the extent that he is a character one can talk about.)

Such drama is a dream
    a lie
    a hypnotic act which has power over fools, (which we all are except at MOMENTS). Such drama is based on inertia, entropy, deadness as conflict works out to resolution—i.e. object, end, death, sizeable "meaning."

At each moment a thing that we "see" (objectify)—Fred, Ralph, Hamlet, etc.—is trying to be itself (Fred trying to be Fred, who desires Juliet) within a system where Ralph is trying to be Ralph-who-desires-Juliet-himself. Mutually exclusive.

So Ralph kills Fred or adapts to being NOT-RALPH-who-desires-Juliet or adapts to being Ralph-who-doesn't-get-Juliet. But in watching this

we watch dead people, sleeping people (as we are in life) and we have
no hint that to LIVE AWAKE is to not-be Ralph—to have a vested interest in seeing and living the
DIFFERENCE
between the inside (Ralph)
and
the outside (events, objects).

Drama (old, what I reject) is people trying to make the inside (their sub-
jective life) and the outside (the world) cohere.
That's a bad way to live, that's a living death.
To live as a HUMAN BEING is to CONSCIOUSLY live the tension
between wish and reality.
All MY "characters"
"do the task"
of identifying themselves with
consciousness
which doesn't (if you will take the trouble to notice
for yourself),
doesn't SUSTAIN objects in the mind (that's impossible for more than
a millisecond)
but presents and represents
in every tiny quanta of time
the content.

Now: furthermore—the overlay of associations
(the harmonies) are DIFFERENT on each re-presentation.
I reflect that.
I have evolved a style that shows how it is now with us, in consciousness. I don't speak in generalities. I show the mind at work, moment-
by-moment.

Most everybody thinks in inherited abstractions, idols (Fred, the sky,
the trees, Wanda's desires, Ralph's personality, love, hate, etc.) so of
course the
REALISM
of my theater seems to be unreal to most people.

The universe as a variation on the theme of the formless (energy) and
form continually interpenetrating each other—now you see it, now you
don't (man: imbalance of inner and outer).

Any art that gives or is based on the illusion of the SUSTAINED OBJECT is bad, unuseful to man's development, his coming-to-himself as a spiritual, shipwrecked-on-earth (in nature) being.

Today, to the man who accepts his split (shipwrecked) nature, the "whole" is only possible as a regressive vision, a kind of primitivism. POSTPONE the whole (as Duchamp's—a "delay" in glass. As Heidegger tells us, we are between the Gods that were and the Gods that will be and must "wait.")

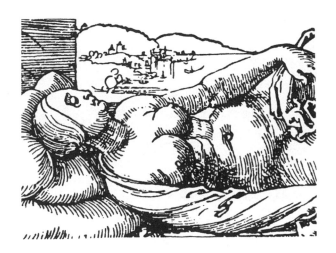

ETHICAL DIGRESSION

1) BE IN TWO PLACES AT ONCE
  (Duo-consciousness:
    Awakedness:
      I.E. The aim)
      2) USING INTENTIONAL PERCEPTION
        (That GRASPS in seeing.
          I.E. The method)
            3) A FIELD OF EVER-MORE-
              SUBTLE DISCRIMINATIONS
                (The necessary
                environment)

To make serious art is to evoke ever-subtler resources
of perceptual discrimination.
BAD art gives us GROSS
                  OBVIOUS
                  OVER-STATED contrasts and juxtapositions.
Man rises (art *can* perhaps help) if he
REFINES
his ability to discriminate ever-smaller differences between
adjacent, or linked, or simply postulated, objects and events.

Our art is the setting up of relations in which one *SAVORS*
the smallest possible differences . . . or the finest point
of identity.
    (1) Match two moments (objects).
        They just, slightly, don't match.
           (the basic human [shipwrecked]
           dialectic between inner and outer that
           are always out of phase, i.e., inner never
           matches outer—no matter how close, how much
           effort: and that tiny, unresolvable mis-match
           [dream and resistance of world]
           [mental image and unexpected data]
           is the source of human creativity, energy, life . . .)
        or
    (2) two very dissimilar objects (events):
        and be able to notice in each the tiny
        seed that is identical.
           (very different objects in which
           the *identity* is subtly determined
           —it being the tiny pivot point between
           inner and outer [the different objects]
           that are always out of phase—but are
           the same in being the two poles of one human
           condition which pivots between them).
Most theater (bad) tries to thrill the sleeping audience with ever new,
ever bigger (gross) contrast (collision, conflict). That merely continues
the process of putting people to sleep under the pretense of waking
them up. "This'll knock their eyes out!" says the artist—
    But it will
    and it will not.

The GROSS contrast between   purple cow and twenty-
                                    foot-high glass
                                    farmer
                                    or
                                    Army of ferocious
                                    Indians and pure
                                    maiden
—these "wake" the sleeper in certain of his centers, which are the same
gross, utilitarian ones used to get through life =
      (sleeping—not noticing deviations and distracting input—so that
      ENDS [making a living, winning the loved one, etc.] can be attained).

In daily life, we suppress awareness, noticing as-little-as-possible of
what would distract us from (inherited, taught) aims.

In art, these GROSS, OVERSTIMULATING contrasts allow us to get
the thrill of "seeing," without real seeing, without effort, without the
need of waking up, without mobilizing the sleeping "noticing, savoring,
intentional perception" that sleeps in us as we live daily life.

      "HALF-DEAD PEOPLE WHOSE PERCEPTUAL MECHANISMS
      ARE ASLEEP TO FACILITATE THE AVOIDANCE OF DISTRACT-
      ING REAL-PHENOMENON ON THE ASSIGNED ROAD OF
      LIFE—HERE'S A THRILL FOR YOU!" (And you don't have to
      wake up to get the kick.)

                    ESTHETICS = ETHICS

The above stated esthetic of gross thrill = an immoral keeping-the-
sleeper-asleep.

Because: everybody should wake up.
      Begin to "see," "listen," "touch," "taste," "smell," in such
      a way that it is
            THINKING (doing those things)
            Not just swallowing.
I.E. NOTICE . . . how (in what *small*: exact [therefore powerful] ways)
each thing that is the same is different and how each thing that is VERY
different is the same.

DO YOU UNDERSTAND THE IMPLICATIONS OF THE ABOVE
DIAGRAM?

NOTICE:
NOTICE:
The art work should be a field for noticing.

Which means: It should *INVITE*
the viewer to *SEE* what's *THERE*.

ART technique has generally been a means whereby the spectator
is *besieged*
by the most obvious possible content available in the
field of the work at a given moment.
    Result—he is so busy receiving (into his
        mechanism) that gross data

        (he has to swallow it)

that he has not the chance to *NOTICE*
to go "visiting"
to "reconnoiter"
to "wake up and explore" the world before him (the
        field of the art work).

So: just as the autonomic nervous system swallows dinner FOR us
        so
the sleeping spectator swallows the proffered sensory input
of gross-contrast art which is AUTOMATIC (conditioned)
perceptual mechanism.

    Immoral art technique (in collaboration with a content
    of gross contrasts) keeps him hypnotized, continues
    to manipulate him in a world of signs—
    rather than perceptions.

The least we could do is to make the content be ever-subtler contrasts and identities so that

When he *sits back* to *receive* . . . he gets VOID!

_____

Then, faced with that VOID, if he wants something to fill it (panic?) he has to call upon, to wake up, the dormant, up-till-now-sleeping

intentional-perception

within. And GRASP—reach out toward, perceptually "make" for him-self—what is "offered" in the field of the work at such and such a moment.

AND WAKE UP.

Just as it's a truism that one only LEARNS deeply when, out of inner necessity, one digs out ideas for oneself,
    so in art
one is only "touched" (touched in an awake state, rather than stroked back deeper into sleep) when the form is such that it invites one (and one co-incidentally discovers the need) to dig out what-is-there-to-be-noticed.

EFFORT ALONE is rewarded; the greater the perceptual effort, the greater the perceptual reward. The art work has to be aware of this and purge itself of the kind of "beauty" that can come and enter the sleeping, passive mind. That kind of received beauty can seem effec-tive but only on the sleeping mind that uses it to sink, through beauty, into deeper sleep.

Beauty that isn't "discovered" or "made" by the spectator in an astute "picking it out" of the field of the work—such beauty is pre-digested beauty that is only part of a language of signs in which "the beautiful" event is another sign—not a disorienting experience demanding human effort in order to come to terms with it and "know" it.

Beauty is only useful or desirable to human development when some-body MAKES it be there by SEEING it in some spot which had been looked at 100 times before . . .
    The audience that RECEIVES beauty

VS
The audience that constructs it, notices it, flushes it out of hiding. Which audience do you want to belong to?

For a long time there has been a certain art ideology which proclaimed that in life one is active, and in art one is passive and receives.
In bad art (90 percent of most art–99 percent of most theater)–
YES.
But in GOOD art–the perception is forced into being an ACTIVE mode.

Good (moral) art (and yes, I dare to refer to those categories) in which–to make it be for himself–the spectator must use active, intentional perceptive modes, has as its end the exercising of those active perceptional modes which might then, someday, enter life itself . . . and transform it.

The test: when the audience says "wow" and they sink into wide grins of awe, or laughter, or tears, or in general have wide-eyed, child-like delighted faces (so loved by the hidden camera which shows people enjoying a show)–

WARNING!

When they frown, and wrinkle the brow, and stroke the chin and say "hummmm . . . curious . . ."

THEN
They're perhaps awake, and working at seeing and noticing how things go and don't go together.

"DON'T YOU WANT TO WAKE UP? TO HAVE A MIND THAT NOTICES THINGS? A MIND AS SHARP AS A MICRO-TELESCOPE?
I CAN HELP
BUT YOU HAVE TO *WANT* IT. WHEN YOU WANT IT–COME TO ME AND I'LL SHOW YOU SOMETHING YOU'LL BE ABLE TO MAKE USE OF.
UNTIL THEN
STAY HOME, IN BED, WHY SPOIL A GOOD NIGHT'S SLEEP."

The result of being awake (seeing):
You are in two places at once (and ecstatic).

Duo-consciousness.
1. You see
2. You see yourself seeing

The *ONLY* justifiable technique in art (art of this historical moment)—
The only technique which is not simply audience manipulation—
(leading the ones who sleep deeper into that sleep)
is
learning how to be in two places (levels, orientations, perspectives) at once.

1) Study all kinds of "FRAMING DEVICES."
2) Study the superimposition of DIAGRAM upon reality.

(Both = two places at once = man's condition. The inner world *superimposed* on the outer [remember, they never quite match and/or they are very-different-but there is a tiny, exact (therefore powerful) common element (pivot point)].)

To be a proper SPECTATOR is to be in two places at once.
1) Seeing where *it* is (the art).
2) Seeing where *you* are (watching).

If you see "it" only—you are not a spectator but you are a person who has been hypnotized.

And you will need bigger and bigger, grosser and grosser thrills, contrasts, effects.

If you see "it" and "yourself"—
If you direct a GRASPING beam of intentional perception at "it"

(which energy beam—like feedback or resonance—then ALWAYS makes you tingle and come back to yourself also and at the same time)
THEN
you will begin to see what most others don't see, and you will find in each inch of the perceived surface—
WORLDS
and energy and delight
and information about how it is in this universe.

(Be assured, intentional perception also reveals
  how awful most art is. It's like looking through
    the heretofore unnoticed make-up of a famous
      "great beauty" and seeing the banality and
        pockmarks underneath.)

To use intentional-perception
to see ever more subtle distinctions
                    IS
human development, and art either serves or retards that development.
  MAKE YOUR CHOICE.
    Have fun if you like, and spend as much time as you like sleeping—
      but realize at every moment, it's YOUR choice, and results will
      follow from that choice.

PART II

For many years I thought the task was to "re-tree" the tree. Make the
spectator see it fresh, strange—as for the first time, not seeing real tree
through the learned concept tree (the standard POUND, RUSSIAN
FORMALIST, PHENOMENOLOGIST idea).

Now I realize—the task is the opposite. Not re-TREE the tree, but
DE-tree the tree. Make it function consciously as the element it *is* in
man's attempt to be a "soul." (To realize what he is—an abstracting
force, a thinking force not IN nature but superimposed upon it.)

The experience of "tree" is a collection of facts—or more a configuration of facts—for instance, turning a corner, looking, being told what's
a tree, deciding to invent a catagory "tree," shade, coolness, rising to
the sun, catching the breeze.

So seeing the TREE is seeing *that* THING out there (being ready
to see it and having that readiness filled)—seeing and knowing you
are seeing that and allowing associations to exist—those associations

which define the tree's being—associations which are abstractions (as memories, possibilities, hopes, projects).

Moment by moment—this is the stuff (these associations, filters of memory, ideas, etc.) that living is made of. Now, the task is to show *this* clearly (the smallest possible unit).

Art should ground us in what-it-is-to-be-living. Not develop our lust for solutions. (And various solutions are: arrival, meaning in the sense of conclusion rather than process, emotion—which once aroused performs a kind of "closure" on the spiritual apparatus.)

Art should awaken a hunger for an immersion in being-conscious-of-process . . . .

Art is a *reminding* technique. NOTHING ELSE. "Don't forget this is going on—an *act* of a certain sort is going on in each millisecond of being an awake, unbalanced, in-collision-with-nature human being.

And most things in our "world" (and most "art") collaborate to make us overlook that process-of-responding-to-our-unbalanced-state . . . and instead we are taught to see objects (rather than perceptual acts) and we are, by those objects, enslaved (desire, envy, worshiping of images). The "object" personality, the "object" beautiful image, the "object" meaningful emotion, the "object" having seen some*thing* clearly: all these make us sleep.

The greatest problem in performance art is how to include digressions, which can clarify, while not losing from consciousness the small event that prompted the digression, which now prompts its OWN digression.

The alienation technique, for instance, is an attempt to deal with this, but a very primitive attempt.

The problem is probably insoluble, but the struggling with the problem is the artist's unique problem and only reason for being.

POSTSCRIPT

One *thinks* about life and sees its richness. Thinking makes life *richer*
  DENSER
    than mere living without reflecting on the living-it.
      (that's why man was
        LURED
        into thinking).

The task in art: to make that awareness of life's greater density part of the pure
    SEEING of it (in each moment—not needing the time-lag-linked "thinking."

> Gertrude Stein says the problem with theater has always been the spectator is either a little before or after his own time in watching, not exactly matching the play's time. That's because pre-Steinian theater didn't have the technique required to make the richness and density be IN the moment, but always asked the spectator to THINK the implications of the presented moment in terms of the past and future moment. Replacing narrative with process-concerns is a way of dealing with this problem.)

Most people like material on stage which is NOT DENSE in the sense we mean, because they haven't used—in their lives—the THINKING that reveals the density of the simplest moment. So to them—
    the DENSE vision
Seems confusion, discontinuity, even THINNESS!
    because it doesn't
                SEEM (appear)
like the life they know. In order to live (in their lives), they depend on various simplification mechanisms that block out everything except the
                USEFUL
          signs, pointers, tools
they find on the narrow road they have made of their life—all energy directed to being able to continue moving along that NARROW road.

(Recall how most modern art is at some stage called SIMULTANE-OUSLY DENSE [impenetrable] and thin [lacking human richness]; this, clearly, because of its wideness—it's open to multiple levels of being [which thought can also, but not simultaneously, discover] and causes the usual, humanistic signposts—which still exist in it—

to SEEM to have vanished, simply because the space BETWEEN
those signposts has been greatly expanded so there is room for

ALL THE REST.)

One should add that the lust for increased DENSITY
of life
Or the lust for SEEING the density that is THERE but
usually hidden until thought reveals it

is desirable because
our being tends to make itself, in the moment
of artistic perception,
isomorphic with the work of art. We get into
the "rhythm" of the music, into the "spirit" of
the novel, into the "atmosphere," "Aura," "world"
of the work of art—its ups become our ups, its
downs our downs, etc.

So . . . being isomorphic with the vision of DENSITY
makes our consciousness SPREAD.

In life—we are on the narrow road of
trying-to-achieve our aims.
Aiming means—narrowing the vision and following
that narrow beam to a goal.

We have to be LEAN and EFFICIENT, and so we
cast off excess baggage. But what is "excess
baggage" on this road toward achievement is
all that is genuinely creative and human
within us.

The great man RADIATES because he is in touch with the (pre-conscious) density and variety and roundness of his being. The other kind
of man is
A NARROW MAN . . . who never leaves the
narrow road and NARROWS
HIMSELF so he better fits
the architecture of the
road itself.

THE WORLD IS ROUND
THE ROAD IS NARROW.
Art should direct us to the world.
ART should REMIND us that one is not an

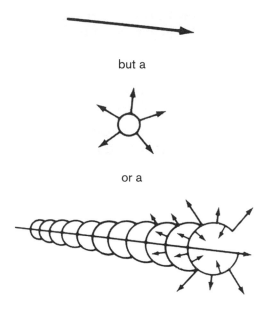

but a

or a

Much art doesn't allude to all that is not "in" it, all the "left out" that is in the world, in thought, but not in the work.

It convinces us, while it is going-on, that "this" is the world.

Most people still reject art that implies "all" because to do that its technique is to have
        GAPS (thru which filters—attracts the viewer's pre-conscious, the "ALL") and those gaps are dissonances, disassociation, discontinuity, dehumanization

and GAPS remind one of what is true:
        That man is always shipwrecked
            That his conscious resources are never equal to his dilemma
                That he will never WIN
                    (Which is different from saying that he cannot
                        PLAY magnificently and joyously—in which
                            case not-winning is hardly a cause for sadness).

But man wants usually to be able to believe that, just like the animal, he is at home in the world. That nature is his proper realm. So to point-out that man is NOT at home—

Well, man can sometimes deal with that intellectually as the "message" So a realistic (which means comforting-style) work can
    tell a story of shipwreck, and sentiments of shipwreck can be expressed
Because man can handle that emotionally by looking at it as ONE EXPERIENCE out of many ("yes," he says, "sometimes we are shipwrecked, but we also have happiness, a mother's embrace, a balmy day, a good meal, the adulation of the crowd, the caress of the loved one"). And so his conscious thinking makes him feel OK even in the face of a momentarily disturbing STORY about REAL PEOPLE.

But to use a style (dissonant, disassociated) which attacks the ongoing world style of assumed continuity and coherence is to attack man's false at-homeness on a level at which he
HAS NOT
the defenses he has against truthful story-telling. Because he is trained to WATCH STORY consciously, so he can defend against it in his consciousness.

But style works on the level of the pre-conscious, where most men prefer to say, "Oh, nobody goes THERE any more," as if it were an ancient vacation place that has long since lost its clientele.

And so style attacks, with truth, where man most deeply is but where he has the least developed navigational techniques. So truth storms
as style
in the pre-conscious
And man *IS* shipwrecked, unable to navigate in that storm
So he says

NO!
To the offending work of art.

And in saying no . . . he says no to what he is and prefers to remain animal-man. At home in the world. Asleep in his mother's arms. Balanced (seemingly). Whole (seemingly). Happy (seemingly).

ONTOLOGICAL-HYSTERIC

MANIFESTO III

(JUNE, 1975)

. . . the process of living always grows out of or is based on certain assumptions: these are like the soil on which we stand, or which we use as a point of departure.

And this is true in every field . . . Every idea is thought, every picture is painted, out of certain assumptions or conventions which are so basic, so firmly fixed for the one who thought the idea or painted the picture that he neither pays heed to them, nor, for that matter, introduces them into his picture or idea; nor do we find them there in any guise except as presupposed and left, as it were, at one side. This is why we sometimes fail to understand an idea or a picture; we lack the clue to the enigma, the key to the secret convention.

—Ortega y Gasset

It is usually assumed that if art has a strong
effect upon us, it is good art, and vice versa.

But a virus may have a strong effect, and yet
be not-good. The same is true in art.

The issue is one of goals, aimed at achievements,
and a judgment or at least understanding of
those goals, plus
the further results, in human life,
which those goals may suggest or implement.

A major goal (of *all* human creatures)
Sometimes conscious, often unconscious
is security.

Art is thought of as man being creative. And the
essence of the creative is the letting-go of what is
in one's mental "possession," so that the
new can arise in its place.

In a sense, the very opposite of security. But I
paradoxically suggest that most art is a (relatively
unconscious) means through which human emotional
orientation toward security-goals are reinforced.

Theater, as it usually is, is a means whereby the
viewer is given the
          FEELING
that he somehow
          POSSESSES
the aspects of life therein treated. He is given a
feeling or experience
          and then thinks of it as something he
          carries around inside himself as a
          memory (a possession).

If, at a play, we experience terror, love, excitement,
sexual arousal, or any other emotion in such a way
that we

ESTABLISH
inside ourselves
a clear LINK

between

the emotion   and the image-situation-
experience that
triggered that emotion
within us

what has happened is that we have been given a memory-
possession which is then available to consciousness whenever
we choose, and we feel emotional stability to the extent
that we have a large number of such items in our memory
bank. We feel security, because each item is an
emotion-linked-to-event package,
into which we *project* that *mastery* felt in being able
to 1) *make* such an internal linkage in
our minds, and
2) call upon it at will for retrospective
savoring.

Such art is not very interesting to the man who wants
to understand and see things as they *are* in their
momentary and unique way of being-present.

I remember
that beginning at age fifteen, going to the theater
every weekend, I would notice even then that most
of the plays
most of them "well received" but experienced by me as
"bad"
manifested their "badness" most strongly during the moment-
to-moment act of watching them.
But a week later the moment-to-moment badness tended
to fade . . .

and certain simple images of the play-as-a-whole which
remained in the memory seemed much
more evocative and meaningful than the moment-to-moment
existence of the play in performance had seemed to me.

As far as I am concerned, that simply meant (and
still means) that
in memory
an experience fades so that RIGOR has no immediate and
exact data to which to apply itself
and so rigor goes to sleep.
It therefore indicated to me (and still does) that the
audience in the theater was (is) experiencing performances
in a way peculiarly different from my own—
since my OWN *MEMORY* experience (a week later) tended to

be in agreement with the opinions popularly manifested
(in reviews, the play's "success," etc.)
—while my IMMEDIATE moment-by-moment reaction to
the material when it was PRESENTED to me was almost
always exactly opposite the judgments and
opinions of reviews, etc.

I now believe that the critics and the public interested
in "theater" invariably see the work before them
through a mental filter which screens out all
considerations that do not reinforce the desired

security-giving configurations of emotion-situation-
idea. And that filter is akin to
      the normal memory filter,
that functions in all of us.
So that most people's relation to the work of art is
akin to one's relation to a thing in one's memory,
i.e., the work is observed in a certain relaxed, receptive
mode of perception
      rather than
an intentional, directed, energized mode of perception.
The work is allowed to seep into one like a memory.
It is not vigorously explored
      IN ALL ITS NOOKS AND CRANNIES
by perception. The relaxed, passive perceptual mode
"overlooks" in the present what it thinks of as trivial
details—much as in scanning a memory the conscious
mind "forgets" what it would call trivial, extraneous
details of past experience.

      But as has been again and again demonstrated, it
is precisely within what one forgets or rejects by
not-noticing that there exists the means of waking up,
understanding, etc. Philosophy, psychology, physics,
—all efforts to understanding—make their great
advances in the same way the psychiatric patient or
the religious initiate does, by learning how to
re-scan the material available to his consciousness
in such a way that the heretofore "unnoticed"
(trivial) leaps out as part of a new, truthful
configuration.

      For reasons related to this, I would go so far
as to say that the STRONG experience in art—the
experience or aspect of it which "stays" with one
powerfully—is suspect. Of questionable value.
      Suspect because its "strength" (recognized and
responded to as such by the spectator) means it is
an "allowed" moment, the consciousness isn't "uneasy"
in scanning and naming it. It is *allowed* to become
a consciously held (owned) memory, and to that extent
reinforcing what we are, our
defenses, our emotional prejudices—evading the
task of awakening our awareness of the implications
and truths of "creativity."

I would say that the most "serious" art, art for
adults, is that which during the undergoing of it
seems rigorous—
   but which after the fact may seem HARD TO
   REMEMBER, because it is (was) that
   which we-are-not-yet, and so
that-which-we-are finds it hard to remember because
that-which-we-are resists . . .
tries to disarm . . . what denies its validity.
   What is important to me in art, therefore, is
NOT the impression one takes away from the work after
the "seeing" of it is over.
   Most people always refer to that after-effect
   and as a result, are always talking
      NOT about the work as it IS
      in its moment of being-there
   but about their own weaknesses in
   perception.

For me, the prime reason for the work of art is to
further UNDERSTANDING (a different understanding
than that uncovered by other disciplines, of course).
Understanding . . . of a very certain kind.

Most theater, on the other hand, is dedicated to creating
an "experience." Sometimes that experience is thought
of as an avenue to understanding. (For instance, an
experience in a politically oriented play, which is
designed to help one "understand" why the workers do
such and such, and the managers do such and such, etc.)

But an "experiencing" does not lead to the radical
"understanding" I am concerned with.
      Here's why.
Experience of any sort is "recognizing." I would not

deny that anything called "art" has to end up in the
thing called "spectator" as some kind of experience.
But there is a difference between this last fact and
the always misguided attempt
     to make the art experience be isomorphic with
an OTHER *experience*-event.

          We experience what we recognize—what we know. Even
if the experience is the experience of "not-knowing"
or "being confused" or anything else to which we
can give a name.

The task of art is to serve understanding . . . by trying
to create a field which is isomorphic with what
          stands-under
experience—which is not experience itself.

          Now, what stands-under experience cannot be experienced,
experience is not the mode by which we can know it.

What *stands-under* experience are the laws (processes)
of perception and other laws-of-configuration of the
universe.

     My task is to make work, the structure of which
     is isomorphic with those laws.

     Then I will be
     standing-under
     experience.

Then the work of art will be an ACT of understanding.

How to find such laws?

They ARE available (Not by experience, but by inference
through the kind of hypothesis-making
followed by "testing" (usefulness?)
which is the basic method of twentieth
century pure science).

For instance: Dirac, Paul. His 1931 theory—
(for me, the most useful MANTRA of our time).
In which he postulates—
Space isn't empty
It's filled with a bottomless sea of electrons
with negative mass (& negative energy)
All available locations in space, filled with
minus energy electrons, no interaction,
no manifestation of their existence!
On occasion, a high-energy cosmic ray hits
one of these "ghost" electrons and imparts
its energy to it.
So, the ghost electron is then bumped out of
the sea of non-existence and becomes a
normal electron with positive energy and
mass.
But that leaves a "hole" in the sea where it
had been. The hole is a negation of negative
mass, so is positive mass (also positive
change).
This hole (DIRAC predicts in '31) would be a
new kind of particle, having mass equal

to and charge opposite to a normal
electron (which is +mass and -charged.) An
anti-electron

But (he predicts) the anti-electron will be
   very short lived because a normal electron
   will soon be attracted to the "hole," fall
   into it, and the two oppositely charged
   electrons will immediately annihilate
   each other.

A year later . . . phenomenon were discovered
which were explainable only by recourse to
Dirac's "dreamed of" theory.

I then dream of the application of Dirac's "dreamed-up"
theory to a different field. (Because I find Dirac's
theory the most evocative, beautiful, moving . . . and
meditation upon its structure makes me CREATIVE.)

The Re-Application

Creation (the act of) leaves a "hole" in the
   world (notice I say world—a socialized phenomenon,
   not universe) of on-going ideas.

The creative moment produces a spark (gesture)
of anti-matter (matter being the on-going ideas which
are the world,

   which are dead husks of far earlier creative moments,
   which
   are the "dead-weight" against which the new, the
   matter against which spirit beats . . .)

The anti-matter of idea being born, which
MOMENT is the creative, is immediately annihilated

by matter—for the minute the creative gesture is
SEEN, is fixed as seeable in one of the
world-mediums that allows representation—at that
moment it becomes another dead husk (*sign* of
something that "happened" rather than the thing-
that-happened).

Now, something *like* this process, which seems to
me to *stand-under* what is experienced, must be
imitated by the play. But it cannot be imitated
except as a process put into operation.

To further verify the significance of the
Diracian "invention" as applied to art—
with the derived implication of the creative
as being necessarily momentary and always
vanishing and always in need of reassertion and
that reassertion being the essence of art,

I give two harmonizing items:

Picasso saying that the artist must put down
what passes through him, with the implication
which follows that the passing through means
a thing arises and dies and in the brief configuration
of its passage . . . (one must die at each moment
to what is, so that one can be re-born in each
moment).

Remembering myself, on the bus about seven years ago
(the Broadway bus!), looking across the
aisle through the window as we passed the coliseum
and trying to see what was happening as I was perceiving
and noticing then and there that much to my surprise,
what was happening in perception was not a sustaining
of what I was seeing or thinking about
even if I TRIED to sustain a subject—but what was
of necessity happening in consciousness was a continual
presentation and re-presentation every millisecond of
subject matter. Even if the subject matter was the
same over a minute period, it was presented, wiped
out in a millisecond, and then immediately re-presented

again and again. That was the way things had
to be in the consciousness.
 (And so, the way things are as-they-are
 for us since for us things ARE in
 consciousness).

And that presenting and representing of item
in consciousness—

That is a process isomorphic with Dirac's dreamed of
way-things-are.

He INVENTED the mechanism that later explained what
 was discovered in the laboratory
And looking at my scripts
 I find
 (my scripts which people have called
 inexplicable)
  I find
the process described above EXPLAINS the way the
units are generated.

   That generation STANDS-UNDER
    the experience

UNDERSTANDING as the aim.

Creativity as the subject.

  Because

That (creativity) is what the subject of all creative
work really is if the work is going to be lucid
and not dealing with glamor or what is vague.

If you write an anti-war play, for instance,
You make an *effort* to show perhaps, what causes
 war, what its results are, etc.
  Now—here comes an audience.
  They are led to see the war was caused by selfishness
which was allowed and encouraged by, for instance,

capitalism. They are led to see the suffering of
the poor, etc.

But in this seeing, which they have been led to,
(like dumb animals are led?) it's as if the author
were pointing away from the real and toward
vague, imaginary shapes and postulates—because
only ALLUSIONS to real information can be made
upon the stage—certainly only allusions to
real information concerning the war and its causes,
etc. The author is saying, "Will you go along
with what I postulate when I postulate a character
like so and so or an act (imagined) like such and
such and an emotion like I *hint* at when I
ask one of the actors to cry something that I hope
you believe to be real tears?"

And as the author is asking the audience to
go along with his POSTULATED reality, he is *ALSO*
asking them

to   *IGNORE*
            &
            OVERLOOK

the real part of the event! On stage!

Which is (the real part) this author's (or
director's) *EFFORT* to *MAKE* this thing (the play).

And that real part is where the audience
COULD possibly discover something
EVIDENTLY true
    not just postulatedly true.

(Notice I didn't say experience something true,
because the *experience* of evident truth compared to
the *experience* of postulated truth reveals them
equal as *experiences*:

An experience is always true and
present as an experience of the one
who is experiencing. And that fact of
experience swamps, dominates the fact

of what stands-
under it.

I said, therefore
  DISCOVER
  something evidently rather than postulatedly
true.
  I mean
STANDING UNDER the experience.)

The REAL part of the event is not the alluded-to war
and social turmoil pictured in the play

but the author trying to CREATE his subject and
  structure—

      that effort, is something more than just
      allusion to ANOTHER reality (the war) that
    has its reality elsewhere and so can
      be treated by the mind in different ways
     but can only be treated by art if it is
bad (i.e., inexact) art.

The subject, if it is the ACT of MAKING the thing we
are looking at—only then is there a

      CHANCE ! A DESPERATE TINY CHANCE !

for real rigor to operate. It's the only subject
(the making of this as it is made)
that avoids the built-in
deadness of the language in which it articulates itself

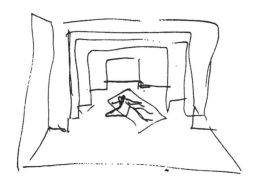

here, uniquely, because language (and I include languages also
    of vision, gesture, etc.)
doesn't have to be something that
    "refers to"
    (therefore distorting what it refers to
    since it is DIFFERENT from what it refers to
    but tries to EVOKE it)
but only spins out itself—web-like—as

its own evidence of what it is, in collision
with what one would make (a play with perhaps
    an ostensible "other" subject).

Creativity (the effort at it) as the subject.

Creativity, which is a spark, always struck, always
    immediately consumed. Immediately struck again.

Creation , the minute *IS* , turns into a
    dead husk. The husk must then be
    replaced (annihilated, as it were) by the
    next succeeding immediate creative moment.

Isn't that a RULE? I follow it.
Isn't that a RULE that STANDS-UNDER?
That's what I want.
To understand.

RHODA IN
POTATOLAND

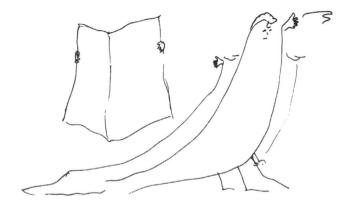

THE ESSAYS

Author's Note

OK. It's about the rhythmic oscillation, very fast, between inside-ness and outsideness.

It's about the tapestry (many threads from many sources) weaving itself and reweaving itself. That process. Each moment . . . a unit of joy coming into itself. Things bleed in unexpected ways into other things. A reverberation machine! That's what my plays are! The theme is the "sequence of things," the theme is "everything that wants to be written"—and how everything is secretly present in everything else.

Also, and more hidden (more *embodied* in the work, like the blood flowing through its veins) there is a certain kind of activity going on in the play—a new kind of activity which postulates thinking as sort of "close to the surface of the body": body mechanisms and manipulations as thinking and perceiving mechanisms and manipulations. A series of manipulations of objects and desires and situations . . . treated by bodies-as-thinking-mechanisms. The plays are about whatever happens when I *am* in a certain way, functioning on a certain level (which gives me most delight) and I open to you in that delight, my joy wants to amuse you with the fact that things inevitably *will* connect, *will* reverberate with each other. *The world is a reverberation machine*, that's what I show you! I allow it to hum even louder than usual by turning, in my plays, away from mechanical casualness. The theme is to document in the plays a certain kind of "constructed" behavior (my invention) in which mentation, mental-acts, take place on an outside surface . . . not hidden away inside. Thinking as the product of field-interchange. The joy of making a thing dance in the mind-which-is-outside, in the body and its field!

Notes on the Process
of Making It:
Which is Also the Object

Understand—it ALWAYS makes sense. Sense *can't* be avoided. If it first seems to be non-sense, wait: roots will reveal themselves.

Anything that is produced, that "arises" on the scene of our on-going human discourse of mutual lived lives, comes from "someplace," from some source—and that fact kept in mind is what orients one to the latent "sense." The sense is what the "arrived" or produced item is translated into by OTHER on-going modes of discourse. No sense is always available, simply a transformation of the "arrived" fact (which makes us see that several "senses" are always mutually available, as several transformations can always be worked upon the "arrived").

The sense of a thing . . . is then nothing but the "old switcheroo" (haha!). Man kills wife . . . BECAUSE . . . (that "because" standing for the demonstration of psychological or social laws, through events rendered—haha! The old switcheroo! Act . . . into IDEA, SENSE!)

POP!
Sense POPS into the action.

Now, if you can be there, on that scene where the sense does indeed POP into the head, where event undergoes its sudden flash-like transformation into idea—to be there on that level, with that process rather than before (in event) or after (in idea) and you will be with me, in my plays, in that place where sense arises (rather than in specific, inhabitable sense or action itself).

Words also pop into the head. Words pop through the web of habitual language, and words that so pop are like ideas. Not words that point to ideas, but words that manifest themselves as an arising of ... a word that wants to be said through me!

and to be there, where that "word-popping-through-AGAINST-habitual-referential-language" is going on—

to stay there on that scene, where that kind of writing is going on

to stay where the old switcheroo is going on, means the writing is alive and speaking from the very center of its energy, of that elusive place where signification makes its choices.

The choices themselves aren't the important thing, but the being-there, where everything is available, where all options are still present, that is the DELIGHT! In the MIND! Where one can laugh and be wise and free and in paradise! which is very important to me.

The sentences I write, which proliferate into a play, are individual doses of acid, hurled against coagulated thought, coagulated feelings, which all stand as a wall blocking perception, hiding paradise. What I am trying to do is get to the grain of thought and feeling. The free-possibilities of the primary process usually coagulates in us into codes, into ever more deeply cut channels, rendering all the more interesting and complex maneuvers and transformations no longer possible. I try in my work to take dictation from the non-coagulated, still-granular source: paradise.

A profound undertaking, but the word profound must be replaced, so that we no longer follow its lead in thinking that the ultimate is a matter of "depth"—but come to understand it as a matter of wideness, greater and greater distribution of the self over the spread network of what is available, the web of everything interrupting everything else upon that surface over which our lives are always wandering.

Therefore, when it seems that my plays, line by line, are changing the subject, that is true—but that changing of subject is the ground of the real subject, an openness and alertness resulting from a "non-human" (post-humanistic) wandering over the whole field of everything-that-is-discoursing to us.

To create as to DISSOLVE into the multitude of contrasting things
that rise up in us.
And so . . . widen.

Most theater is narrow: dramas of intensity

> like an arrow, a route, a hypnotic trance.

> Our interest is a granular widening, a spread-
> ing, a stretching of attention itself, so that
> attention is a globular universe on the
> verge of popping, fragmenting. But in sus-
> pense. Focusing on all potential fragments
> equally at once.
> Not progression (which is hypnotic) but sus-
> pended, alert, free.

My art embodies (yes) a setting to dance (to work) in that place
where the play-is a certain kind of attention that doesn't, like normal conscious attention, sink all else into rejected non-attended
un-consciousness, but a certain kind of attention, like a cloud of
agitated particles, bounces, reverbs, smacking into all, agitating all,
leaving the trace.

My art as an awakened, empty, singing way-to-live
   (but the brain does the singing
    the mind does the singing
    not the human-nature part of the self).

A model then, for a way to live the good AND THE bad:
         ALL the contingency
         ALL the interruptions
             errors
             stumblings
             changes of subject

Meaning is ALWAYS (inescapably) "there"
Multiple and spectacular in its
      many shapes and facets.

(One of the most interesting aspects of my work is the way items
(sentences, acts, adventures) generated through so-called non-
willed methods . . . are allowed to melt into each other so as to

cohere; the way I lay back and frame the thematic configurations that inevitably take shape. The way I let writing itself prove, demonstrate, its inevitable drift and/or bunching up into meaning. The thrill, the delight, the joy of seeing that law of "drift to coherence" have its way on stage as in the mind and heart.)

> Produce a field
> in which
> Objects . . . haha
> are trivial.

> BUT THE FIELD IS IRON!
> RAVISHING!

To create that field (rather than allowing the consciousness to be hypnotized) my plays keep "changing the subject." But is it changed? Since the subject is the field, not spoken of directly, but articulated, laid out, by the writing of "things."

> The pleasure I take (writing) is the pleasure of undercutting: interrupting: an impulse I want to (and do) make. The impulse is registered, but allowed to twist, turn, block itself, so that blockage, that reaction to its energy, produces a detour, and the original impulse maps new, contradictory territory.

> The impulse is the explorer-consciousness, staking out new claims, finding a way to be self-generative, not simply reactive.

On purpose, on the root level of expression-of-impulse, I try to get into the greatest difficulty possible. Syntactically, logically, rationally, narratively. "Train-of-thought" trouble and blockage is cultivated.

The center of the work is in that trouble, stumbling, drift, in that resistance to all "effort" which is, I maintain, the source of all reflexivity. That "coming up against things" which is the experience that forces us to "see."

Divergence from text.
Write the divergence from the center.
Write the meandering, the wandering of the writing
as the writing covers a territory.

The current life-game (current perceptual styles,
    emotional habits of living ones sociability, syntax of allow-
    able mental moves) doesn't seem to allow what I consider the
    potentially most interesting moves.

My plays, therefore, postulate, for me, a PARADISE where the
"allowed" mental move is the move to undercut all impulses, to
self-block, to strategically change the subject, so that a desired
emotion is produced—

    that emotion an invoking of the feeling of
    the infinite
    the infinite in each grain of sand
    the infinite (and open) in the small cell of
        each "moment" of my plays (since each
        cell is an item "X" that generates
        its own multitude of non or anti "X"s).

The resultant music, hum, that the field of the play so generates
is, for me, a paradise. A gymnasium, in addition, where kinks are
worked out of the mental muscles so that all those "more interesting moves" of mind and spirit are increasingly possible.

To undercut
thought of as changing the subject (people say my
chain of non sequiturs). But IS the subject really
changed? If what is evoked is always
the emotion of the infinite moment in the grain (unit)
of sand (play): That tension?

    Art refreshingly, exhilaratingly, thought of as an aid in teaching
one new navigational abilities.

Old inherited navigational abilities we all share to a greater or lesser
extent include the ability to plot one's course through cause and effect,
through metaphoric systems, statistical modes of organization.

I'm proposing that there are new ways to navigate which I'm trying
to be-in with my plays. Very hard to define, but I can HINT by saying "quantum jumps," by saying "parallel rivers of discourse, one or
another intense at different moments, can you jump back and forth
between those rivers and the HARMONY of that jumping."

To be, to write, in such a way that the MARK is not a continuation
but a change of direction, a twist, a displacement.

Something that was left out.
To write before writing: To make the writing
the preparation for writing. humm . . .
I MIGHT write such-and-such
I MIGHT write . . .
I MIGHT write . . .
I MIGIIT write . . .

So there isn't progression or development (19th century edifice
complex: impressive what man can do) there is rather—like the
electron—a "being potentially present" in many places at once.
Structures of potentiality, not heavy, massive edifices.

And the staging like that too. It MIGHT be staged to mean THIS
. . . a kind of attention . . . but invaded, immediately undercut,
by THIS DIFFERENT shape or realm of discourse or object or
rhythm.

Breakfast . . . invaded by geometry
geometry . . . invaded by desire
desire . . . invaded by houses
houses . . . invaded by a direction . . . or
other "not identifiables"; simply rhythms, qualities, etc: And
that cross-reference to different discourse systems.
The energy of that jumping, that shifting, is what DRIVES
thought. My plays not ABOUT THOUGHT, but ABOUT WHAT
DRIVES thought.

Like energy released by a quantum jump.

Trains of discourse being jumped. The play tries to BE-WITH
that, EMBODY that.

The real subject of the work isn't WHAT is articulated but the condition of

being-there-with-the-articulation (that saying or writing or
staging when energy comes into its expression)

and being-there also with what NECESSARILY (that's life,
folks!) undercuts
    twists
    displaces
       that expression

(being-there-with means embodying in the work rather than talking-
about in the work;
NOW we are doing the talking about, but in the art we find it more
interesting and exhilarating and "truthful" to be-there-with.)

—————————

I am interested, then, in an art
which STRETCHES, WIDENS, the mind's configuration.

A good "classical" melody of a certain sort . . . spreads us, with its
"unexpected" next note (compared to popular jazz or ethnic music
which usually takes the more "expected" next note in order to hypnotize rather than spread attention.)

That energy present to us in each moment, can either be focused—
which is to say "used" and exploited by the hypnotic object or
developmental pattern (easing us down the melody with increas-
ing speed and intensity)—or it can become "spread" . . . distributed
energy. Awakening, as it were, a whole field of mutually interacting
particles.

The WIDE, SPREAD configuration of self: (the wise self)

It's not a matter of *confronting* a wide field

It's assuming a mental set
                posture
                configuration

                of wideness (open to
                      interruption, leaving doors
                      and windows open for it)
                no matter what the size or
                particular nature of the
                field one surveys.

Art then as a tool. To perform leverage on the head and its habits,
set the head to work somewhere else.

Bad, boring art tries to convince (usually in the realm of feeling).

Good art . . . can't convince of anything because its method is to interfere with (undercut) itself. The task is to be with—equally— the impulse AND what interferes with, undercuts, stretches, tumbles, dishevels, scatters . . . the impulse.

To allow interference . . . is to allow the wedge . . . that moves the mountain (the inertia of where-we-are).

Our art does not "speak" of this . . . but rather EMBODIES this. To speak of such things is invariably to drag the new back into the language of the old . . . and the old language is always (we are habituated to it) always more "powerful," more "seductive" to our mental mechanisms, than the new insight.

FINALLY: To understand in my plays, keep watching the "cell" of the moment. Try to watch *all* that is present in moment "A," and then *all* that is present in moment "B," and so on down the line.

IT'S LIKE POLYPHONIC MUSIC. YOU *CAN* LISTEN TO THE MELODY PLUS ACCOMPANYING CHORDS, but that is NOT THE REWARDING way to listen. The music is really to be heard as a sequence of chord modulations; you should listen vertically, to the SPREAD AND TENSION OF EACH CHORD, then succeeded by ANOTHER SPREAD-OF-NOTES-PLAYED-AT-ONE-TIME "CHORD," and so on down the line.

So in my plays, it will help you to watch the cell in its complexity and "spread," then succeeded by another cell, and another.

THE IMPORTANT THING TO REMEMBER—it's not the development from cell to cell, but it IS thematic modulation, continual thematic modulation . . . not to carry you deeper into being hypnotized by your own emotional habits and responses . . . but to maintain a certain sort of mental & "feeling" tension which will keep your faculties "spread" to the optimal degree (the best, most energized way in which to care for your head!)

FULL OF FEELING—BUT NEW FEELINGS!

So it should be clear, the work aims to *be* in a kind of paradise.

> Where a series of moves
> in the game of using-the-head
> which are normally NOT-CERTIFIED as "standard moves"
> are energetically indulged in.

And that exercise, of making those moves, will slowly change the "game" itself . . . and one WILL be in paradise!

How Truth . . .
Leaps (Stumbles)
Across Stage

The first thing to say is that I believe in the efficacy of false starts. For the past tcn years, the work that I do in the theater has been built upon a structure of repeated false starts in the belief that the gesture, the impulse, which comes to nothing (which doesn't fulfill itself) . . . fulfills that other thing which is truthfully operating through me . . .

Now, the theater—which is my less-than-enthusiastically-embraced home—in its relation to the spectator, classically equates truth with the power to convince. Something in the performance (emotion, style, invention, rhythm: SOMETHING) . . . must be what we call convincing—which is to say "masterful." Such mastery . . . becomes aesthetic truth. The emotion convinces that it is real emotion; the stylistic cohesiveness convinces that its fabric hides no holes, etc. Even with the evoked interplay of illusion-and-fact of modernist theater, the theatrical production tries to convince of its mastery in that manipulation.

Now I believe, of course—or, I find it interesting to operate under the assumption—that that need of the theater to be effective, to be convincing, to testify to "truth" in such a manner . . . is the heart of the unavoidable corruption and vulgarity of theater. I believe that convincing my audience of anything—ESPECIALLY of the effectiveness or intelligence of myself as an artist, imprisons and degrades that spectator so convinced. One reason I believe this is because I find myself, in my own work, imprisoned, hypnotized, fooled whenever I do something well, whenever I am (to myself) convincing in my mastery. Because at that point I sense I am, myself, hiding from truth behind the façade of the well-built artistic edifice. So my work has been, over the past few years, to document my failure to really live up to the rigors of that impossible situation where one must show that all mastery is anti-truth.

The truth is . . . when any artist makes something—even if it's only an Artaudian cry—that produced thing is an effect of deflection, or distance . . . away, not from any hypothetical source, of course, but away from that temporary nexus where the always overdetermined strands of cause meet and cross. So whatever I, as artist, make . . . is a *falling-away-from-the-truth* artifact; which—to the necessary extent that I'm not 100 percent strong and honest, I improperly try to re-direct toward that fallen-away-from-truth . . . by falling into the trap of trying to convince you, my audience, of SOMETHING (ANYTHING) about SOME of that object's qualities.

I'm claiming, then, that truth . . . seeks out art so that it can experience a turn against itself (or away from itself) . . . and in that departure of truth from itself, and ONLY there . . . productivity and proliferation are possible.

And all the while, I—congenitally dishonest like all artists—try to recoup truth by convincing you something about some aspect of my artifact. It doesn't matter what aspect, just ONE of the many. And that aspect about which I try to be convincing . . . Is, clearly, historically later in time than any of the innumerable overdetermining causes that were at work when the first impulse toward that artifact began to function.

But you might well counter that claim by maintaining that the truth of the artifact . . . is its functioning now, in concert with whoever is perceiving it, is that network of assumed messages back and forth, etc. The interesting thing is that in that case—as opposed to an artifact which convinces—i.e. MISREPRESENTS itself, i.e.—lies: we then have an artifact which at least potentially dissolves within the multitude of messages in which it participates.

OK. That's desirable. Yes, I *DO* think that some sort of *dissolving* of the art object—which is invariably dishonest in its need to con-

vince, is desirable. But what seems most interesting to me is to dissolve the art-work as self consciously as possible. Myself, I'd like to
build it into the object . . . in such a way that my actual making of
the work is a *being-there* with the dissolving process.

I believe . . . or dream . . . that . . . the siren call of truth re-directs all
my effort . . . over the years . . . to this need to dissolve all mastery,
all effort that leads (implicitly) to mastery. I seem to spend my life,
as we all do, employing that biologically given mundane energy . . .
making efforts. And after I've made such an energy driven effort . . .
I feel satisfied. Good. Making an effort, the feeling good: feeling as if
I've accomplished something through effort, that feeling lures me,
I believe, in a direction opposite from truth.

Let me say that I am . . . and I consider this my constituting "am"—I
am lazy. When not directing a play or film, I find it very easy to
fall into a passive, receptive state. And indeed, speaking of truth
(speaking casually, so truthfully) I feel that passive, lazy state to be
the TRUTH of my particular character. I'd rather have things easy
than HARD, and I find it difficult to believe other human beings
want it otherwise. Yes—people want challenges, so that they can
meet them in the hopes of achieving and FEELING mastery and the
ease that brings. But it's all aimed at . . . that ultimate relaxation.

Now, in that passive state, which I feel to be the truth of my character—I feel I am connected to the truth of myself as I am *NOT* connected when I am active and producing. But paradoxically, the truth
of that character "ME" who is passive—is the truth of a character
who is *NOT* connected to the truth, because only effort and rigor
and building makes that truth—retrospect—at all available to that
character. I have to construct something . . . something . . . to see
how far it takes me from myself. And then I have to return to myself
. . . denying (or dissolving) what I've constructed . . . in order to BE
IN the TRUTH.

So here I am, stuck with a self who believes that to perform is to
be less true to oneself than to be passive. Nevertheless, I believe
that performing, which takes effort, is desirable . . . in that it makes
a kind of field . . . where truth can accidentally show its traces, its
path, as it trips over some irregularity in the constructed field. And
I end up believing that truth only reveals itself—or at least leaves
evidence of its having-passed-through, when it stumbles. And one
sort of stumbling is . . . truth turning against itself, distancing itself
as the lie.

Now, generally, the field itself hides truth, for generally any field which causes truth to stumble . . . is, as field, itself so dense, seductive, CONVINCING, that it distracts us from that slight indentation truth makes in it. The field—the art-work—is dense to the degree that it is, on some level, convincing. And that field . . . that CONVINCINGNESS . . . must be dissolved.

The way to dissolve that field and yet, paradoxically, leave something where truth's indentation is visible . . . the way to do it (and this can't be done, simply can't be done) . . . is to *fail*. To make a work of art a failure.

Discourse, coherence, convincingness—have to fail. That's the method.

You have to start out speaking . . . in the art, and then let it drift, fall apart—so that a begun trajectory splinters, gets lost.

Lost, unseen, and therefore convincing nobody, not even yourself, you do the work of truth. Which is the work (related to overdetermination), which is the going-out in so many small deflections and splittings, that no one person follows even a fraction of them. To sink into REAL unconsciousness. Like a knock-out blow, to get hit on the head . . . or what is better and easier . . . to fall asleep!

Ah. Perhaps a secret method to put people to sleep! The worst thing you can say about a performance—it was so boring it put me to sleep. But what a fantastic dream . . . to send an audience to where truth is REALLY at work!

It's interesting, because now I remember what I hadn't of course forgotten, but hadn't till this point even thought of saying. Something relating to my writing procedure. This writing now (that I'm reading) . . . is coming out of a certain effort of will. And that is NOT the way I proceed when I write—or as I prefer to say, GENERATE . . . a text for the theater. Now today I have the obligation of saying something—and I've been looking to find that point where I will be seized, carried away by the writing.

But in writing my plays . . . I DON'T WANT to be carried by the writing. I DON'T WANT to be taken away . . . moved . . . away from the truth. And though it's impossible, the dreamed-of temporary solution is, as I'm writing, giving up . . . which is actually . . . falling to sleep. Falling to the depths . . . while not moving from the spot.

I generate my plays, allowing contingent truth to begin speaking, and then I fall asleep into it. Literally.

During the afternoon, I'm lying down on my couch, reading a bit, making notes, my books and papers propped against my recumbent body, half covering me. My hand makes designs on the paper . . . a brief bit of dialogue is scratched across the corner of a page . . . and then, eyes glazed as I write . . . I fall into a light sleep. After five . . . ten sentences . . . I shut my eyes to rest them, I feel my head expand and empty . . . and then, I'm asleep. That is . . . I dissolve . . . where I am.

When I continue writing, perhaps the next day, perhaps later that same afternoon, I don't remember what writing has come before. Time and sleep and other things have dissolved that previous writing inside of me. I never go back and re-read it. Now . . . instead, the material is circulating inside me, invisible. But also . . . it does trip me up. I make sure of that. Because when I come to put the play on stage—months later—I find to my surprise that a certain sequence "B" follows another sequence "A" in the text, and while they are or are not accidently related in some way—they invariably DO trip each other up!

They did not, during the writing, expect to be next to each other on the page as indeed they were. They did not expect to be next to each other, sequentially, on stage—where now they are about to fall over each other. (Owing both to their inherent nature, and to certain strategies of my mise-en-scène.) But still my personal problem, pursing this lurching forward of truth through my landscape . . . is that in front of the audience . . . I have difficulty in accepting the ultimate responsibility of putting that audience to sleep in front of my play. Of letting them . . . be on their own. In their OWN depths.

I also . . . like other artists . . . fall again and again into the trap of trying to convince you of something or other on stage . . . to convince you at the very least of my mastery.

It is true that ten years ago, when I began, my work on stage was very slow and static and might well have put my audience to sleep if they would have agreed to stay in the theater long enough to have it happen to them. But I couldn't go on working that way forever, and my current practice is to attempt to have speed, pure speed, do the work of dissolving my theatrical objects: trying to go so fast on stage that one cannot really perceive; trying to invisibilize the field in that fashion; dissolving the field in that way, so that it *IS* like sleep. Sleep . . . in another concretized, three-dimensional form.

I have to assume that in my dreams I'm not lying to myself. And I think it's possible that if I go, when awake, so fast that I can't follow . . . then, whatever lies I may be telling counteract each other. Speak beyond themselves. But, of course, it doesn't really work. When I make an art-work, like anybody else, I'm still only building a road AWAY from . . . not a source, but a certain . . . something else.

And a question is—if one wants truth—can the road circle back to its starting point? And I believe it cannot, because as it goes, it splits, branches, and continues to do so until . . . everything (both out there and back in here) becomes only road. It's all filled space, filled with road. So theoretically, you can be everywhere all the time, which is the real . . . fantasy of the artist.

But I don't achieve it, of course. So the most truthful thing I can do is to FRAME, to EXHIBIT, the traces of failure. Then I'm WITH THE TRUE, if not in control of it. And I have to dissolve the field where this occurs . . . or else you (and I) will believe in that FIELD as "the truth"—which it *IS* as function (it that causes the stumbling) but which it never is as object. In order, as an artist, to really BE WITH this process . . . I believe I have to be so sensitive, so unfit for living, that I—or truth in me—stumbles over the smallest imaginable speck of material. That really does mean to be unfit for living. And that's the only way I believe my work could really be with truth.

But . . . I'm not good enough to be that unfit for living. Because either my personal mechanism isn't under my full control . . . or else it *is* under my control and indeed *THAT'S* the problem. So I court incoherence, but I don't quite make it. Because however incoherent I become, I'll always—I see—be able to leap across to a new position, and then comment upon that incoherence from that new, OTHER perspective. And the truth . . . as I tumble from one position to another, will always be falling out of my pockets, like loose change . . . falling to the bottom of the hole, of the emptiness, over which again . . . and again . . . I leap.

The above is a transcription of a paper delivered at a conference organized by the Italian Psychoanalytic Association on the subject "The Truth" in Paris in May of 1980.

14 Things I Tell Myself when I fall into the trap of making the writing imitate "experience"

1.

The art . . . aims to reflect something that "stands under" experience, rather than experience itself.

Each situation we are in, each experience, quivers with the different
    not-yet-known-how-to-use
ways in which the materials of that situation might otherwise be combined, organized, set to work upon each other.
Against that free-play of elements as a backdrop, one (in life) makes one's choice of act, thought, gesture (a choice always rules by the need to echo, imitate or extend previous choice-patterns in order that that choice shall fit within the pre-defined limits of the rational).

But! It is those continually REJECTED choices of the backdrop, never articulated yet always present as the un-thought "possible," which give plasticity and depth and aliveness to what is chosen.

Our art then, to discover the secret of liveliness, shows by example

not—what choice to make (as does all theater which imitates
   "actions")
but—shows, concretizes, that which—though it cannot be chosen
   —stands under what is chosen, so that choice is alive and
   energized

The not-thought, the purposeless, which nourish all activity
and experience. The acts of the play are then a series of
acts and gestures not-chosen in life, which for that
very reason serve as the roots of life's (or should we
say consciousness's) liveliness.

2.

The audience must watch not the object, not the invention,
but the way in which the object twists, is displaced,
distorted.

But the important thing is to realize there
is no agency responsible for this twisting, this
distortion—there is a groundless displacement which
is the very source of the play's meaning, and the
very seat of consciousness (concretized by the play) itself.

This groundless twist picks up the objects at hand
and fills them for a moment, gives them being for a
moment, and then lets them fall back
into the sea of the non-manifested.

This groundless twist is the energy without a source
about which we cannot speak—only ride its back as it
were. The one choice we have is either

   seeing and experiencing—which means
   having no contact with the generating energy

   or standing-under seeing and experiencing,
   and so being where energy is; mis-matched
   with it—but the double condition of
   being-there and not matching (i.e. distorting
   it) being the only real condition
   of self-reflexive "knowing," which the play
   —also mis-matched but being-there, knows.

3.

Our art then = a learning how to look at "A" and "B"
and see not them
    but a relation
that cannot be "seen"
You can't look at "it" (that relation)
        because
it *IS* the looking itself.
That's where the looking (you) *is*, doing the looking.

4.

The compositional principle is NOT
                  anything goes
                    but
only write that which allows itself to be
deflected by the world (which world includes
the act of writing, of course).

Most stuff you might write wouldn't be so deflected
(and so must be rejected). Either it would be too porous,
the world going through it without deflection;
or too heavy, it wouldn't budge—or it's in a sealed room
where the world doesn't even notice it—hence no
contact and no deflection.

Writing is also the invoking (of the gap, the mis-matching,
which is where we *are* as consciousness, and which
is a force). The invoked energy or force isn't what
gets written. It arises, then in the staging, but it
isn't in the staging.
The writing invokes the force *WHEN* that writing is then
staged, so long as that staging is such that it *allows*
the force to come. The staging doesn't make it (the
force) but the staging gets the writing (which is the
original invoking) out-of-the-way in the proper way, so
that then the force can be-there.
The force IS disassociation, consciousness, displacement,
a groundless "twist" . . . so it is there and not there. It is
"other," it is "possibility" . . . not as a category, but as
a force.

5.

Writing has not a subject
> (aimed for)

but is a being-responsiveness, to the currents
> within it as it generates itself. "It" is
> writing thru me, and it is doing *other*
> things also so try and show those other things.

It's not the item; it's how one slides off it,
> leaving a *rent* in the fabric.

Theme: that slidingness: which can't be said, because
> to say IT would be to *not*-slide off *IT* being said.

6.

One must find ways to sacrifice "what comes" to one
in the writing.

> Offer it up . . . to what Gods?

Destroy it as useful to use in daily life as-it-is. Rather
serve it up to the elsewhere in us.

> The play is then a ceremonial ground. Certain operations

are performed. Not to tell (you) something. Not to take
(you) elsewhere. But an important and significant
activity goes on
which you watch or not watch.
But it isn't there for you or for me, it's for the
benefit of someone else, hidden within us both, who
needs to be fed so that everyday you and me can still
be alive in a way that has plasticity and aliveness of
thought and perception. Understand, it's not a question
of refining the GOALS of thought and action, but of
keeping the process itself grounded in a kind of energy
that makes the process itself want to continue.

7.

In writing (as one takes dictation from what wants to
be written) the received is twisted. It (the received)
looks at itself through the twist (which is yourself) and it
(not-you) gets a sense of itself and proceeds.
And then that which proceeds . . . is received, twisted, etc.,
and the process continues and a text is generated.

8.

I'm lying on the bed.
  Looking toward the window.
  The curtain moves in the wind
    A motorcycle noise in the street stops some other
    process of watching going on in me.
    I write that down.
Desire plays through me for a moment.
Music from a window across the street and the sound
of water running in the tub.

  A level. Everything level for a moment.

The writing is a certain thing
The action of wind, etc., noticed but not thought about, is
a certain thing.

The writing is imprinting
  a certain noticing
  on a certain existent system.

It never matches.
  That's why displacement is a rule, and a generative
  principle.
           o . . . . o

I make a model for the way it is.
One can't express the real experience.
  Experience is one kind of making.
  Saying is one kind of making.

  The gap between is, of course, the source, the fuel.
  Mis-match
    Displacement.

So I don't (try not to) notice thought
But rather the gap between experience and thought
                input   output
                passive   active
         What I write (notate) is the gap.

9.

The plays are about what they do.

Which is to concretize (show) a certain sort of
system which goes-on in me.

In which lived moments . . . are open to displaced
energy which is objectified as an energy that wants
to handle and penetrate the object, and that handling
and penetration twists, displaces,
distorts the object (which is the lived moment).

As a result the lived moment is denied as a self-sufficient
experience . . . and re-constituted as an energy-
exchange which, as it leaves the evidence of its being
on the page being written, is no longer an experience but a
mark.

      In the beginning: the mark.
That mark, that concretized evidence is, for me, heavier,
denser than experience itself. The play is an energy
diagram in four dimensions. A condensation of what
goes on in me, objectified.

I don't make pictures evoking the experience of things,
but notate what circles through us, leaving
a residual grid that makes experience then possible
(registerable). That grid . . . made intense . . . is the
work of the play.

Experience is then burned up, petrified, sacrificed on
that intense grid of the play.

10.

Within the play as an object, there must not be
"A" theme, because one theme or meaning closes the doors
on all others—and ALL THEMES AND MEANINGS MUST BE
PRESENT AT ALL MOMENTS.

      The organization of the composition should dis-organize
the ego (which is what wants a theme to be-at-home in) and
evoke in the self the dispersed self (in which ALL themes
are).

(Simple dada & surrealism don't do that. Nonsense,
irrationality, don't do that, they don't dissolve the ego,
they are rather anti-bodies which, injected,
strengthen the ego. They wall themselves in from
the world as non-sensical or supra-sensical, which
only increases the need and ability of the ego to
define its territory as against "external," irrational territory.)

The OBJECT of the play, then, is to make the spectator
be like the play
(or recognize that he *is* like the play).

I am like the play.

(We are what interferes with us. Result, a kind
of self-knowledge. But whose self-knowledge?
There is no *who*. Only knowledge.)

11.

Always, at the beginning (which means finally) a sentence
wants to write itself.

Then, that sentence suggests a next sentence, because of
habits of association, because of a world in which we
are trained, taught that one thing must lead to another,
that there are paths to be followed like responsibilities,
etc.

To escape that:
Write the sentence that wants to be written.
But then pull away from it—or from the inherited
        associations and commands and rules that
            cling to it.

Pull away from it. Let something that interferes . . .
        twist
        the sentence, as it emerges or in the next moment,
        as you look at it.

There must be no theory of writing. The writing is
the phrase or gesture that floods one and wants to be written.
But then, there must be
        A theory of what to do after the writing has
        had its way and written itself as a word or sentence
        or sentence cluster.

The 1st moment:
   What floods one. Then, twist it. Find
   ways to inhabit it, plant it
   in the world NOT as a tool,
   not as a lever to move the known in
   known ways, but to turn it into a
   self-reflexive item, around which a
   whole new world crystallizes.

The 2nd movement:
   In staging . . . interfere. Let
   the sentence be so crystallized,
   become so intensely itself, reflecting
   itself . . . that interference actually
   FEEDS it
            strengthens it in
   its clear uniqueness by being
   not-it in a subtle and
   interfering way.

12.

The choice is to discover what is (clarity) by *seeing*
desire at work (not simply letting desire produce, because
its products often cloud seeing).

There is a choice—either seeing desire at work
or
   Form production (which is to cover over what-is with
   "what should be").

Make desire-energy produce a structure that is self-reflexive.
That is, make desire as it produces, produce the right
form, which is a form that will see itself (so that *we*
can see, through it, since the desire is *us*, what-is-there).

Is that not form production? Not really, because we
   are not speaking of willing a certain form and
      then "using" desire to fill it.

We are speaking of working on the desire itself,
   through conscious displacement, distortion, employing
   a strategy of identifying with what-interferes.

Then . . . what is produced has the "right" form whatever
the form of what-is-produced. Because when the desire
is producing . . . through identifying with what
interferes there is a displacement, it doubles itself
and so mismatched it sees itself. And the play is isomorphic
with that activity of twisting, splitting—looking at itself.

And the play at work is clear, not producing a form
but producing a doubling, a displacement which is a real mirror, and
clarity.

13.

The meaning is in the suppositions that start one:

In my case, small bits of experience and thought interfered
       with—
how the unconscious and the world (the same) get-in-the-way,
and how that interference is allowed.

The text = strategies for allowing the world to interfere.

       And making that interference one's own, as an
       oyster makes a pearl of the interfering, irritant,
       grain of sand.

Now—what is interfered with is NOT a project, or
       aim, or narration

but just being-there in one's self.

       If it is a narrative or project that is interfered
       with, then the self is still there.
       But interfere with just-being-there and the
self is dispersed.

14.

So . . . Each moment has a different meaning, each moment a
different theme. The piece is about making oneself available
to a continual barrage of meanings and themes, so that
one is transformed into a being
       spread, distributed
a different configuration of the self.

The composition always implies, no, no the meaning is
not here, but elsewhere, spread. The piece is always
pointing away from itself. Meaning is equally distributed,
everywhere. Classical art, everything is focused in on
a certain theme, points to the center, each moment
cohering. Here—each moment takes off in a different
direction.

The unity is the procedural way of turning away
from the center. There is displacement, continual
replacement of one meaning with another.

There is a sequence of a certain sort of item, called
"possibleness of manipulation." There is a straining
after certain figures that the mind-as-a-body
wants to articulate in space.

Exemplary titles: *Book of Levers*
                     Action at a Distance

Theme: Showing that mental acts take place on a surface,
       not in the depths.

Depth as the ultimate fantasy. The ultimate
evasion. Linked, of course, to a concept of
center. So de-center. Displace. Allow thought
to float up from the depths and rest on the
surface. Look at it . . . handle it. Match
your life to it . . . as does the play.

The play, finally, must be fed and "controlled"
by a multitude of sources. As many as there are
"sources" of experience in one's own life.

That multiplicity, acting in concert, becomes the
"unity" of the process of continual displacement. Only
work to make sure no single displacement escapes
the immediate interference which must arise in the
next moment, allow no single displacement to begin
to build a wall around itself and form its own
kingdom, its own order of being. Such a
kingdom or order would be a return to the sleep
of experience within which most art keeps us forever
imprisoned.

The Carrot and The Stick

My method of procedure in generating texts for performance hasn't really changed in eight years in at least one rather peculiar way. I keep sending myself orders on "how to proceed"— reminders of what I'm aiming at, and piles of these orders accumulate on my desk next to the notebook filled with the scratching that eventually gets shaped into a "play." What I REALLY want to be able to stage someday are these obsessive theoretical out-pourings— but I don't know how, yet . . .

One does not think words, or sentences, or acts, or stories— but only, wherever you are at this minute, waiting to make something—twist, and that twist is, somehow, the unit. And the work is built out of such units.

A certain rhythm of interruption and shifts on a repeating "frame."

(Frames, too, alter, but are always frame-like.)

The art . . . must be isomorphic with the feeling aroused by itself. That means, chasing its own tail, which means in turn perpetual motion. The feeling comes after the art which causes the feeling, and yet the art which causes that feeling, made isomorphic with the feeling—and this all conceived *not* as a temporal process. But somehow learn how, in the instant, to shape the moment so that it will be resonant to whatever effects it will produce. Then, when the effect *does* occur, one is truly able to perceive the "structure" of that effect. That's what we should build—models of effect-structures.

Usually, feelings are aroused and out of those feelings one acts. Hate is aroused, murder results. The act *issues* from the emotion. How much better, to discover within the emotion, some sort of framework, along the struts and supports of which one can align one's body, one's imagination, one's gestures—so that the "act," rather than issuing from the emotion, etches its rather imaginary configuration in the materials of the real world. (The motive, of course, not change, but lucidity. The spiritual motive.)

About four years ago, I discovered how, when suffering from a headache, to lie down on the couch and stop "fighting" the pain, telling the headache to "expand" as it were, until I was alone in a center of a vast web of the throbbing pain—and somehow in that center was a stillness and the pain—no longer resisted—vanished. In the same way—try to generate in the text certain points that are "bad" (whatever that means) in a way that the pain of the headache is bad, and rather than trying to fight to eliminate those points—enter them, let them (the badness) inflate like an entire world in which you can find an entire structure within which a whole life of rigor, passion and intelligence can be lived. The end may be slightly different than the end of "headache elimination," but the starting point is the same. A relaxation and allowing of "bad" material to expand to the very horizons so that *I* am on the inside of *it*, rather than *it* being experienced as a foreign agent within *me*.

Trying to be centered . . . on the circumference. Something inside of you (like a headache, or your response to a "bad" line of dialogue) is a feeling. Relax and let it expand to the horizon, then you are alone at the center. The feeling . . . has become the structure (world) within which you move. Then your movements (your art) indeed become isomorphic (you move along roads laid down by the expanded feeling) . . . with the feelings they, originally, created!

I've always wanted my art to be *about* whatever it was that gave me the energy to make it. My works, therefore, are a mode of literary criticism, in which the object under analysis is itself.

Most literature expresses how the artist feels about a certain sustained "subject." I invariably choose to express how I feel about the preceding moment of generated text. Mostly, how I feel about the energy that generated that preceding moment. Or rather, the relationship between that energy and the one out of many possible ways it chose to crystallize itself. Continual judgments and reflections upon what just was "there." So the critique of the play is not so much built into the play—it is the body and flesh of the play. Indeed, the critique of a play that isn't there—and I feel the play *shouldn't* be there, because if it were there—it would only be there for the *moment* of its performance while what would remain (forever) would be the memory of performance in individual spectators' minds—that memory (selective, judgmental, *etc.*) immediately a form of critique, and so I chose to make the work out of "what-it-is-that remains" rather than what is momentary (non-existing). So what is articulated and organized is not so much acts, as responses to and reflections upon acts.

To understand the work, one should not, of course, ask what it "means," but only—what need does it answer. In my case, the most consistent, passionate need . . . is the need to FILL A SPACE in which I find myself (mentally). That is, I suppose, a kind of erotics of thought . . . using thought to manipulate the imagination, which is a body. Fill that space (where one is now, and then now, and then now) not by being at the center but rather by a twist administered to the imagination-body: an un-natural extension of some sort, generating a new periphery, a difference.

We lack a center, always. By definition (man). It's wrong to try and provide a center (the play should imitate what-it-is to be a self, which is to be centerless). We are peripherally defined creatures. Joy and exhilaration will be attained in the work if it imitates what we really are, which is a process involving a lack at the center which receives a collection of in-mixed traces, so that our mental antennae are constantly feeling out to the "edges" where we imagine those traces to originate. Don't, therefore, think of filling the "space" of the moment, but in the moment distribute oneself at the periphery. That would be a union (of "X" with) *other* codes, traces. Then let that union, that in-mixing be the agent that does the acting. The "I" doesn't act—the generated sentence, the gesture that results from fold laid back upon fold, the idea that appears as a wrinkle where one line of input stumbles over another—those are the agents of the "act."

My experience continually (life experience, making-art experience) is one of "hummm, that's not quite right" and I try to back away for a new angle of approach, and be seized, there, away from my center,

inspired (which means jolted out of line, twisted) by a trace, other-
ness, irrelevance, "error," which in speaking through me will, as it
were, change the rules of the game.

The irony, which is still at the motivating place of the drama, simply attacks different "objects" these days. With the Greeks, it was
the irony of an act producing a result opposite to its intention (will
effort followed by reversal and revelation). From Shakespeare to
Ibsen, the irony was relocated in statements, where a statement is
made and can no longer be believed to say what it says, because
we know the character is lying, or pretending, or calculating. Now,
the irony is in the very *field* of discourse. It pulls the very sentence
apart. There is no longer a speaker, towards whom an ironic perspective is to be employed . . . but the total field of words, gestures,
acts available to the "speaker"—each "item" in that field is now perceived as ironically meaning its opposite, causing its opposite to
"be" the minute it is performed. That is the modern, ironic, consciousness. The performing (or naming) "A" evokes (invokes) in that
instant, immediately, non-A. It is only against the field non-A that
A can make its entry. We KNOW that. It is one of the few things we,
in this historical period, know in a more *lived-in* mode of knowing
than men of earlier eras.

Poetics of production:
1) A "meaningless" event.
2) A field of experience.
3) A point of view relating 1 to 2.
Think of life as a "music" of these three interpenetrating moments/
realms. The borders between them shifting all the time, of course.
An item "A," could shift, oscillating between 1, 2 and perhaps even 3.

     1   2   3
Listen-speak-click of release that's no-mind. Ah!
Learn-create-objective letting-be. Ah!
A possible sequence:

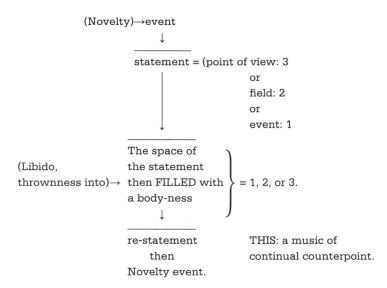

(Novelty)→event
↓
_____
statement = (point of view: 3
                    or
                    field: 2
                    or
                    event: 1

(Libido,   The space of
thrownness into)→   the statement
                    then FILLED with } = 1, 2, or 3.
                    a body-ness
                    ↓
_____
re-statement   THIS: a music of
    then   continual counterpoint.
Novelty event.

The most interesting task is to discover the *shape* of the now-moment. So it becomes a matter of forms, more than a matter of structure.

What is the form of the present, and each succeeding present? Then, see what-can-be-done with the form that is the real form of the here-now. Those here-nows as the building blocks of some other structure. But the quality of the blocks determines the possible "style" of the overall structure.

Now, the form of "now" can be determined only as I try to twist my body (mental) until it FILLS somehow the moment, till it touches the borders of the moment. The meaning, then, cannot be in a superimposed fable, but is in the modes found of—"being able to inhabit" (fill the spaces of the present, and the sequence of those modes). Meaning is—"How do you live in a space?" Spaces arise, the way mutations are delivered upon the planet—and then life tries to inhabit that new, mutant species. In the attempt to make an arisen space "habitable" (a species is also a "space" for living)— meanings arise, such as, "That plant is poisonous." I am concerned with such meanings.

Meaning? Make an item (the play) that other items can allude to when they are making an effort to crystallize their own meaning-to-themselves. The play doesn't allude to a real world, through having a "meaning." Rather it is there to "give meaning to" anything *else* that wants to take meaning from *it*.

What we need are models for a "way-of-being-in-the-world" that we'd like to remember as a possibility. I'd like, myself, to be "tuned" to the world in the way the play I create is tuned. I establish the world of the play so that hopefully, I can turn to it, and begin resonating to its rhythms.

I generate a text, I make a composition out of what I "know," that is to say—a collection of "meanings" carried around inside me. One meaning . . . in conflict with another meaning. That means, of course, a continually shifting frame of reference. That means of course . . . that there is no conclusion . . . no beginning, middle and end . . . but, intermissions. Until I die. But then I won't be able to write about it.

In the work of art, you are never talking about what you are talking about. You are always using talking-about-subject-"A" to really talk about subject "B." But most of the audience doesn't understand that, which makes of the theater especially a rather absurd undertaking (if you would make art). Why do I do it? Well, I had my reasons, but I'm not sure I'll do it much longer.

One reason one makes art is to have more control than usual over what goes out and into one. Because if you are making a work of art, you devote a significant number of the available hours of the day to controlling that input and output. So the work of art is always a picture of one's ideal world, a postulated utopia. But again, it is not the "things you are talking about" which constitute the content of that utopia, those "things" are used to talk *really* about something else. So the utopia—there, before your eyes—is unseen by most people. Why both talk about what you are talking about? Ah—to talk about it is to first catch it, so that it can be "displayed" (talked about in theatrical language). To catch it, to make it hold still, you have to kill it. Everything that is talked about (displayed on the stage) is a dead thing. I don't want to "kill" what I REALLY want to talk about (utopia) so I have to talk about OTHER things I don't mind killing and then those dead things are talking about other things that somehow—because they don't have to be "displayed"—don't have to be killed.

To EXPRESS something means you first killed it.

One can hardly help generating things that give pleasure. We are built to "take pleasure in." But the effort must be made to try and insure that pleasure will feed not the "I" (which should be the developer of will) but rather the disassociated not-I within us. The not-I is both a more sensitive, subtler, more intricate pleasure-experiencing machine than the I—and the sole field within the person which will NOT degenerate through repeated pleasure stimulation. Clearly the "I," the ego, does so degenerate into sensualism if fed too rich a diet of pleasure. But inside of us there is all that "passes through us" (the other, which is always threatening to disrupt, the selfhood we feverishly hold onto) and that "other" in us takes the pleasure it is fed, breaks it into a hundred small pieces, and sends it flying to feed different parts of that energy system which because it is always challenging the coherence of the inner "I," forces us to new efforts of will and invention.

How to feed the "other" in us (the not-I, as opposed to ego) with pleasure? Ahh—but everything in this collection of notes is really speaking to that primary end, dealing with that primary problem.

Ritual as anti-doing, the anti-pole to force (see Erik Gutkind). My life of writing is a ritual, I make nothing through force. I copy certain things (or, let rise certain things) and that doing-so renders me transparent. Erases me as a "force." My work . . . erases me. So, I am not. What I am finally, is a part of the composition that arises through me.

We can postulate two (of many) systems going on inside us.
1) A "receive perception" system (always a clean slate).
2) A memory store.

Those are "imagined" systems, suggesting new ground rules for the game of art-making. As opposed to such an imaginary system, there is a more verifiable neurological bi-part system in which
1) Certain neurons PROTECT us against the strength of incoming stimuli.
2) Certain others receive stimuli.
The fact is that we pick up the frayed ends of system 1 on system 2. So I can suggest to myself—write the PROTECTION against noticing, generate gesture of defense against input.
Also:
The perceived may be read in (on) the past (the memory slate upon which past perceptions have left their imprint).
"Pure" perception would go in, and vanish, and be not.
Real perception is resistance to perception.

Can you imagine what kinds of texts, suggested by above proce-
dures, might be generated? Would they not resemble my texts?

Old paradigm: Universe consists of forces that solidify into units
(Gestalts, objects, events) to which we *respond*.

New Paradigm: Universe consists of forces that leave traces which
are not fully identifiable consciously, of which we see only residual
evidence—and if we respond, it is an "error" of responding to what
we *project* into those traces.
If you believe 1, your art tries to make something visible, and the
life copied by that art is a responding-to-input from the "world."
If you believe 2, your (my) art tries to erase things (because they are
obstacles) and the life copied by that art is a "something else"
that tries to resonate to inner output.

The TREE of senses.
Man is currently the "seeing" creature—that sense defines him
vis-à-vis other creatures, who have more highly developed
"lower" senses.
Smell (taste)
Then: hearing
Then: seeing (man's current level)
Then: thinking (the next level, not yet achieved).
THINKING . . . as a sense. As a way to respond to what is present
. . . by THINKING what is present, rather than smelling, hear-
ing, seeing it.

So, try to make a new art about THINKING—THINKING treated as
a *sensing*, as the sixth sense!
Try to imitate (anticipate) the next stage in the evolution of
consciousness. What that amounts to is a planned opposition
(within the work) or restriction
of organic releases (pleasure): which is also a way consciousness
could be thought of—a restriction on immediate release in sensation.
Past achievement of man: to turn "tree" into a sign, which can
be held in the head. That's what men have achieved—symbol-
making, sign-making ability, in which conscious experience
mediates between man and encountered tree.

The next step might be to restrict the emotional release man now
gets through his encounter with signs, and so see the sign (object)
dissolve into a kind of web-of-association awareness. See the signs

become nothing more than polarity-traces. That web-conscious-
ness then mediates between man and signs and he no longer sees
the "signs"—just as in encountering the tree in the field, he no longer really sees the "tree." Instead of the tree—he flashes the sign in
his head "tree." So in the future—he no longer flashes the sign—but
the entire web-of-associations and differences in which tree-sign
occurs as an item.

Then: thinking . . . as a sense. In the way that "seeing" now mediates between man and experience—separates him from experience
because it translates outside into inside—so thinking could be a
similar translator . . . KNOW THAT, and make the ENJOYMENT of
that be the art enjoyment. Because to separate himself from nature,
and then from experience even . . . seems more and more to be man's
destiny! Man *is* the abstracting animal. Keep going.

      KEEP GOING!

New York, 1975

How to Write a Play

**(in which i am really telling myself
how, but if you are the right one
i am telling you how, too)**

make a kind of beauty that isn't an
ALTERNATIVE to a certain environment
(beauty, adventure, romance, dream, drama all
take you out of your real world and into their
own, in the hope you'll return refreshed, wiser,
more compassionate, etc.)
                                but rather
makes GAPS in the non-beautiful, or look carefully at the
structure of the non-beautiful, whatever it is (and remember that
structure is always a combination of the
                        THING
                        and the
                PERCEIVING of it)
and see where there are small points, gaps, unarticulated or un-
mapped places within it
        (the non-beautiful)
which un-mapped places must be the very places where beauty
CAN be planted in the midst of the heretofore unbeautiful.
        Because the mind's PROJECTED beauty (which is the only beauty)
        . . . can either find itself in the already beautiful (so agreed
        upon) or it can MAKE
        Conquer new territories.

But: while in the midst of the heretofore still un-
redeemed "non-beautiful" the projection of the will-to-beauty
can either be a pure act of will in which there is a pure, willed
reversal of values
    (which can have great strategic value but creates art that DOES
    tend to "wear out"—not, you understand, a negative judgement)
        or
    our method.
    find the heretofore un-mapped, un-notated crevices
    in the not-yet-beautiful landscape (which is a
    collaboration between perceiving mind and world)
    and widen the gaps
    and plant the seed in those gaps
    and make those gaps flower . . . and the plant
over-runs the entire landscape.

What this amounts to is a DECISION
to view non-beautiful material in such a way that what was
    foreground is now
background . . . and the desired beauty is then projected, as the creative act, into the midst of the heretofore rejected (non-beautiful,
un-interesting, clichéd, etc.).

——————————————

Delight is delight.
It aims us to whatever it is that delights us.
Can we make a more CONTROLLED use of that energy of "being-
aimed" by willfully choosing to have a certain object be the one
which arouses that delight-energy? ANY object?

Of course. That's the task—discover how to be in control, how to
CHOOSE
which object shall provoke the delight phenomenon

(and so increase that per-centage of the world we can say "yes" to,
and thereby gain an inexhaustible fund of "delight-fuel").

Here's how.

Normally, let us assume we are delighted by a sunset
    We are not delighted by a corpse.
But if we place the corpse within a certain composition, let us say—we
are then delighted by the composition of which the corpse is a part.

So—while we are still not delighted by a corpse, we can be delighted by something (made or found) of which the corpse is a part.

The task of art is to find what heretofore does not delight us, and make that part of some kind of composition in such a way that delight results.

Now, the composition need not be a composition in the expected sense, that is, need not be something that is defined or defines the art work itself—

The composition may be any "context" in which the material is placed. In much art today, for instance, the context-composition is "the inherited history of Western art." So that the reason a minimalist gesture such as a Morris black box is "delightful" is because we understand it as an intelligent next move chosen in the context of an evolving "game" which has been the game (move and counter-move) of Western art.

So in the theater, which is always behind the times, one must ask, "Ah—what can we include in the on-going context composition which heretofore has been de-valued and kept out, etc., etc.," and few people in the theater ask that question and do that thing and so the theater is rarely art, and when it is it creates problems for itself since its audience is not an audience interested in art but in entertainment.

Which means, its audience is interested in being delighted by what they already know in themselves as delightful. And their response to the attempt to include NEW material in the composition—material which they heretofore have categorized as non-delightful—their response is generally negative because they have never been trained to be composition perceivers rather than object perceivers. When they look at theater, they use daily-life perceptual modes and so see things, and not patterns and contexts and compositions.

The rallying cry must be—stop making objects that men can worship.

Art shouldn't add new objects to the world to enslave men. It should begin the process of freeing men by calling into doubt the solidity of objects—and laying bare the fact that it is a web of relations that exists, only; that web held taut in each instance by the focal point of consciousness that is each separate individual consciousness.

In my work, I show the traces of one such web. (The assumption herein is not idealism, because the consciousness is a constructed thing also, on a different level subject to the same laws of configuration as the world outside, a collection of trace elements, not a self-sufficient constituting agent: but the relation between consciousness and "world" is the relation between two intersecting force fields, neither of which is a thing, both of which are a system of relations.)

I show the traces of such web intersections—and by seeing that, you are "reminded" to tune to your own. Find objects in a sense interchangeable (and, in another sense, poignant for that reason). But most of all, find exhilaration and freedom and creative power, for when you see the web of relatedness of all things—which is in a certain ever-alive relation to a "your own web" of consciousness—you then are no longer a blind, hypnotized worshiper of "objects"—but a free man. Capable of self-creation and re-creation in all moments of your life.

Most audiences and critics want to be moved, knocked out. That is a sign of their illness, blindness, need to remain children. Most audiences want a perceivable, nameable content. That is, they want to be able to reduce the experience of the work to a gestalt of some sort that they can carry away from the theater with them.

That means, they want to feel that they have extracted property, capital, from the investment of time in the experience.

NO! The art experience shouldn't ADD to our baggage, that store of images that weighs us down and limits our clear view to the horizons. The art experience should rather (simply) ELIMINATE what keeps us moored to hypnotizing aspects of reality.

Or better—by showing how reality is always a "positive" which is but a response to (an extraction from) a "negative" background, it allows us, in terms of this continual, now revealed polarity, to make contact with the reality that is really-there. Not by social fiat, but by operating at the constituting heart of things.

It is not a matter of getting BEYOND, DEEPER, HIGHER than everyday, normal, agreed on culturally-determined reality, it is a matter of—within the confines of the art experience—allowing ourselves to partake of the "taste" of a perceptive mode that strategically subverts the very OBVIOUS aspects of the gross and childish conditioned perception used to "browbeat us" through life. The gross mode of perception that suppresses the contradiction at the heart of each consciously posited "object."

The artist must search for what has never been seen before.
   BUT
Not simply a new "monster." Not a new "that knocks me out like . . ."
(a pyramid, Shakespeare, sex, etc.)

But
a new
object which once found
is hard to see. Maybe it's not even "there."

We live in a world of traces. Things leave traces. We must never try to make man believe that what is by definition constituted as a "trace," has indeed a different kind of reality—that of "object."

The emotion must never come, as it usually does, through our being convinced of the reality of the image or event presented, but only the ecstatic emotion of one's own seeing of things. Delight in one's own energy.

NEVER awe or delight in the "worshipful way" we feel emotion when we are awed or moved by the "other" which seems like an alien other in which we "wish" we could partake (all romantic art).

Need for Confrontation

Art + = to CONFRONT the object

Kitsch =　atmosphere replaces object. Distance between you and object de-creased by atmosphere which makes you FEEL at one with the object because the atmosphere is felt to be that exuded by the object. But then object and you (feeling) are one and there is no ENCOUNTER, and no seeing. (To play the subtext, rather than the object, for instance.)

What is the object? The encountered object, encountered in making the work: the "real" chair, body, word, noise, etc.

The constructed object. The end with (art) is the STRUCTURE of the articulating process. The MAKING A THING BE-THERE AS ITSELF (in its web of relations). Process.

The artist doesn't explain, analyze the object . . . but he sets it up so that one CONFRONTS in the realist fashion its BEING-THERE, which is a confrontation to your own BEING-THERE.

PARADOX

The way to confront the object is to allow it its own life—let it grow its own shoots in directions that do **not** re-inforce its being-in-life for use as a tool, but that suggests a compositional scheme not centered on useful human expectations. So, let the chair that is for sitting have a string run from it to an orange, because if chair was just "chair for sitting" we would not "confront" (as we not-confront in kitsch) because we are too close to the chair, its meaning is too much OUR meaning; but now chair-connected-to-orange is an "alien" chair that we must CONFRONT.

> (To reveal an object or act, gesture, emotion, idea, sound.
> To make it seizable
> To speak its name you must
> make it part of a system not
> its own. Involve it compositionally with
> another realm, which is YOUR realm of pattern-
> making isomorphic with your
> mind-process. THEN there is confrontation.)

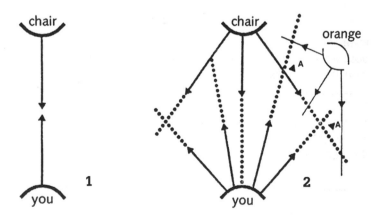

KITSCH	ART
(and sleep) as	(and awakedness)
the moment of	as
contact between	the moment of
you and object	contact between
is one dimensional	you and object
and you are	is multifaceted and
in a state of	often "distant" (point A)
identification	from the object.
(hypnotized by)	
with that face	also
of itself the	in 2 (as opposed to 1)
object presents	your mind-pattern-
to you.	process is being as-it-is:
	and THAT structure
	inter-acts with the
	object structure as-it-is.

In 1 the mind forgets
its own working and there
is no real meeting, only
a 1-dimensional (1 "presented"
face to another) moment of
"official" (clichéd)
    "something"
that is too mindless: i.e. one-dimensional
(lacking points "A" of 2)
to be a real encounter.

Diagram 2 explains, once and for all, all of my plays!

The message must be "To choose either turbulence or serenity is an error. To choose either knowing or doing is an error." So . . . in the play . . . inject disruption into knowing, and order into passion.

The play is a lecture in which you don't say, "This is so . . ." but rather . . . "This occurs to me and it occurs to me that the reason it occurs to me is this act, which occurs to me," and so on and so on, deeper and deeper.

My message is "filling the space with the idea." Free play within the idea. Ability to treat the "field" of the idea as an area for work and discovery. Idea as a field . . . in which something that is not idea (but more physical, sensual, ecstatic) can emerge.

I write to make life handle-able.

The deflection inherent in time. Space—
one makes art to be able to decide what goes into you
                          and what goes out of you.
    To be in control of what goes into you and out
    of you is why you decide to make your own art.
    Of course . . . as it goes in and out, space and time
    give it an uncontrollable "twist."

Lived experience is a certain kind of focus. You focus on an aimed-at while living, and because you are focused on that, you don't see your own gestures. Art: is trying to see your own gestures.

My gesture has always been to pull away, to change what came into me, to make something BETTER that could then go into me instead of the thing that did go into me. Hence, to find a way to make better FOOD for myself than was provided by others. My art then (one's art) is a way of being-in-the-world so that the INPUT is the best possible input . . . into me.
Journalism is trying to imitate life. Art is an amplification of the effects encountered in trying to make art.

Art: a machine to effect input. To provide awakening, energy-giving discontinuities. To fight entropy. Art is NOT comment on life. It is fighting the entropy of life-that-seeks equilibrium, that seeks not-stress, which would lead (as life does) to death. (Inject quantum shocks, discontinuities, to keep twisting us away from sleep, death, into what is "artificially" sustained . . . AWAKENED LIFE, CONSCIOUSNESS!)

Form in art—form isn't a container (of content) but rather
    a rule for generating a possible "next move."
        That's where the subject is (in that next move, dictated or made
        possible by the form). The commonly-thought-of content or
        subject is the pretext to set a process in operation, and that
        process is the real subject.
The text is me
It grows like I grow
It extends itself, falls, stumbles over . . . something.
    Recovers. It projects itself as it will. Encounters resistance of var-
    ious sorts, but those resistances turn out to be steps affording a
    new advance
stretch extension twist
Stage it: try to make the compositional aspects be
in relief. The **structure** as it were. Not the structure
in time, but the structure of the moment.
    (Time doesn't exist. It's all now.
    There's memory-now-future.
    Now doesn't exist
    It's a pivot point
    Make things structured in that pivot point.
    (I.E. frame now, frame not-there)
People who work in time are making things for memory
    Are not clear about here and now
      Proper analysis here & now
        What am I doing now
Man is future-oriented, but life is collision in now between project
and what resists it
So: each movement shows what interferes with, contradicts, projects—from other levels. Not just conflict of people. What contradicts the "play" itself and its mode-of-being-present.

    That privileged object which is the ONE object that must be
studied . . . (so that man can study what it is most important he
study) . . . that object is not yet "available." Not yet there.
    In making a play I am trying to make that important object that
is not yet there.

How I Write My (Plays: Self)

To write about my writing . . . which is, of course, what I write about, sort of, when I write plays.

It's a matter of the life I live, at certain moments (how are those moments determined?) cresting into a moment of writing.

It's a style of living, at certain moments folded back on itself to produce a style of thinking; at certain moments folded back upon itself, which leaves a residue (look, look! the hand moved over the paper and left something!) of a certain style of writing.

The life should be described first. But bear in mind that the life has, for many years, been adapting itself to a certain obsessional need to get something onto paper, to AMASS a certain kind of material on paper, which would, hopefully, as the MASS grew, suck the life itself into the orbit of the being-style manifest in the writing (which crests aspects of the living one hopes to change) . . . so the process is circular, spiral, pulling oneself up by the bootstraps.

When I am not in active rehearsal (at which moments I am full of energy, focused, highly alert) I tend to lead a certain kind of lethargic existence (yet with a certain kind of alertness ready just below the surface—like an animal dozing, who can yet awaken at the slightest "signal" of the appropriate sort).

To be specific, I lie about the house, alternately reading (either skimming pages for "what I need" or reading POWERFULLY to twist what I read to my own needs), making notes (I spend a good part of the day with pen in hand, almost as an appendage, ready to JOT DOWN either notes, ideas, quotes from reading, or bits of dialog or scenes which will be in a play) and not infrequently, dozing off. (I should add, perhaps, that the reading often involves looking at pictures of one sort or another; I should also add that the NOTETAKING also involves making a multitude of small diagrams and sketches, both to clarify and map out what I've been reading and thinking and to project or imagine a relevant "setting" to what I've been writing or thinking.)

The writing itself is a cut taken in that tunnel of passivity. The entire process of making the play thought of as a certain and continual articulation of alternately passive and active modes. The writing tending towards a more receptive, open, passive receiving of "what wants to be written," and the staging tending towards more active organization of the "arrived" elements of the writing—finding ways to make the writing habit a constructed environment, just as a passively "arrived" species mutation finds a way, after the fact, to exploit and live in the environment in which it finds itself.

It should not be assumed that my day of writing, and within that the writing done on that day, can be thought of as exclusively passive. Indeed, an important aspect of the process is the way in which the "drift" of time and effort allows for eruptions of specific willed activity. I often begin a sequence (to be sure, that beginning the result of "having an idea" one wants to see carried out, the process of most writers, implying a kernel of receptiveness at the root of all art, even the calculated organizations of an Ibsen or Scribe) I begin a sequence "willfully" . . . and then, if it tends to "lose the energy" and peter out . . . that truth of process must be allowed to stay in the text, documenting that 95-PERCENT-OF-THE-TIME-MOST-IMPORTANT-FERTILIZING-FACT OF MENTAL LIFE (that most projects come to naught but are nevertheless the substructure of most so-called "achievement") after which, as Stein says, "begin again."

The writing is then the documentation of the exploratory will, which "receives" ideas, turns them over to look at them, subjects them to its very personal and idiosyncratic method of investigation, and, in so doing, EITHER receives another new idea for investigation . . . or does not. (It should be pointed out that in addition to the possibility that the received idea peters out, another "ending" for a unit which I frequently experience is a kind of premature closure in which I start with an impulse which I have the feeling opens a potential "world" for exploration—and then, somehow, after a few sentences or exchanges, I am already at the other side of the territory, having the feeling of "covering it in a single step": OK—begin again!)

Some will now interject, "Oh, but then the plays are not really structured at all!" I would maintain that such an opinion reveals a gross misunderstanding of what is involved in the making of art—an extremely narrow view of what constitutes structure, even "willed" structure. You see, I have been working on the machine of myself for a good many years now—or, to be more exact, I have been working on the somewhat more complex machine "self and circumstance" in order to adjust that machine so that it will, when the starter button of "good morning" is pushed, turn out a certain product which will have a certain "effect" on a certain kind of human attention— should that "certain kind" of human attention happen to come in contact with the product (my plays) in question.

It is my belief that at this moment in time, this sort of structure, spun by the articulation of the whole of self and setting, produces the "tool box" most suited to the task of performing the necessary leverage on the head and its particular collection of ideas. It's less a matter of a structure which will appropriately "package" ideas so that the consumer will be able to "get them down his gullet" (the classical modus operandi of art) but rather a structure which will force (or be there to "assist") the spectator into a new position vis-à-vis the continuing barrage of input that constitutes his life.

I say that I have spent years working on my machine—it should be clear, for instance, that the considerable amount of time I have put into writing manifestos and other articles delineating and figuring out for myself the theoretical implications and next steps for the kind of art I found myself in the middle-of-making reflects this attempt to get my consciousness into a place (through a mutual adjustment of daily life and writing) where it will IMPRINT with great directness and truth the "faulty" and yet "wondrous" mechanisms of its inescapable and continual digestion and transformation of impression-and-experience nourishment it receives from the world each day.

Why did my machine start working in this particular way? Well, there was a sequence of events which was roughly as follows:

1) Being a very shy kid, being taken to the theater by my parents, and being so attracted to that world of make-believe that I wanted to copy it and be in it, which I did start doing at about 8 or 9 years of age, making and staging and starring in my own copies of Gilbert and Sullivan, discovering, through making it, a world in which I could

both "dream" (escape) and at the same time function with
an AUTHORITY (as director-producer) not available to me
in other aspects of my kid-life.

2) Continuing with a career of actor and set-designer-
constructor through high school and into college; but my
taste widening, being hungry for the most "experimental"
work I could then find or imagine because only in that work
was there the hope of occasionally finding moments, tones,
colors, which seemed to match the contradictory and complex nature of reality (internal and external) which I was
fast discovering was not "officially, institutionally" admit-
ted to exist by the educational and social systems by which
I was being processed.

3) In college, beginning to write because friends who were
"writers" would come and ask my opinion of their latest
effort, and suddenly feeling "I can do better than *that!*" My
writing, then, after a year or so, beginning to be the writing
of plays—because I basically wanted to justify myself by
becoming "famous," and being a famous playwright seemed
OK. So, imitating everybody from Arthur Miller to Girau-
doux to Williams, Sartre, and finally Brecht. By the time
I was at Yale (studying with John Gassner) I was regarded as
"professionally promising"—prided myself on my "vicious"
intelligence, which I felt could take apart whatever needed
to be taken apart, and, like most professionally oriented
playwrights, delighted in my ability to not-so-much write
as REWRITE plays so that they would "work" on stage (i.e.
so the actors would find the kind of material with which
they—and the director—could manipulate the audience
through a desired sequence of emotions and emerge at the
end with a nice, not too simple but not too subtle, "meaning"). It goes without saying that at this time my writing
habits were to get an idea (after searching around for the
right combination of theatricality and political or psychological or sociological relevance), then do an outline, then do
a first draft, then rewrite and rewrite again until a) the style
seemed polished and strong and b) the plotline seemed efficient and rose to the proper climaxes with the proper eddies,
swirls and theme-refracting detours along the way.
　　At this point the writing was coming out of a highly
active mode of self, in which a great deal of willed effort

went into making what the superego determined was right and professional and IMPRESSIVE, a great deal of effort into rewriting to eliminate what did not seem "right."

4) Coming to New York and meeting Jonas Mekas and the independent New York filmmakers movement and discovering a new esthetic, built upon a truthfulness in attempting to catch the natural rhythms of the individual artist—come-what-may as a result. The big turning point in my art, learning to accept and make central to my work the very elements which I had heretofore tried to suppress and exorcise as not being "weighty, serious, impressive" enough.

5) That watershed reached, developing independent exploration of the themes and possibilities available to myself and my circumstance. Coming into the full realization that there are two ways to approach and serve art: a) the creation of structures which aim to "impress" and hypnotize and further enslave people to their own emotions and ideas, or b) the putting-to-work-of-a-way-of-dealing-with-materials which embodies a sort of high and lucid and, therefore, deadly serious "playfulness" which can stand as an example to inspire both the self and others to ever-greater exploration of what, momentarily, is—*opening the door thereby to both freedom and creativeness.*

So now, a day begins and I have pen in hand and I am doing all these things—reading, lying about, thinking, sketching, jotting things down, not knowing I suppose exactly where I'm going but knowing which road should be taken because the only OTHER road that has ever been pointed out to me has led, 150 times in a row now, to works of art which occasionally have their moments but which basically both bore me and (I would maintain) are subtly enslaving those who "make the effort" not to be bored by what they already know to be true (i.e., their own emotional responses to murders, loves, betrayals, righteous indignation in the face of injustice, and all those other fine things that classical art is always "about").

Now, all these concerns about which I have been speaking—at every moment in which I am available to do any writing—these concerns are hovering in my mind, and the writing that I do is written against that background. And it is not very EASY for me to keep myself oriented to those concerns, because they contradict the habits of my early training in school and society—and to fight, fight, fight those habits at every possible moment is my concern, and that has to be done by me consciously and rather continuously, and that effort sometimes bleeds onto the page on which I am writing as a little injunction or reminder to myself, and I allow that to stay in the writing (the play), too, because—can you see why? It's such a deep and important part of the whole effort. And can you see why the invoking and allowing of the passive mode is part of the effort—to allow in everything that I was originally conditioned to KEEP OUT! So the will, the directed activity of my "writing habits" is to keep ME, RICHARD, in a place where what I now consider the "good" writing will come from.

It is true—even now I feel frightened to admit this, it's going to be held against me as a sign of "lack of ultimate seriousness"—it is true that I no longer rewrite as I used to. It is true that I keep and then stage what appears on the page of my notebooks. (Though it is also true that when the time comes to mount another play I always have much more material then I can use, so I do select in that sense. But the material I choose to stage is always taken in sequence as it appeared, without deletions.) But this is not, I maintain, to stage "unedited" material (though God knows, that would be a perfectly justifiable and important artistic procedure also).

The material is highly edited, and it is my specific writing "habit" which does the editing. As I see it, the lying around and reading goes through and is twisted by the head machine and comes out into a different part of the head and is therefore "writing." Only it doesn't get onto the page which, staged, is the "play." So that's "writing" which is edited (pre-edited) from the play. Then there is the continual hum of thought, which is being written and most of which doesn't get onto the play's page—even though, remember, the pen is always in hand, paper always near and ready to receive the least twitch of a tendency toward actual, physical, ink-on-page writing. One of my plays speaks of "writing out of low energy," and what this refers to is the fact that I have been concerned to develop a writing habit which demanded the least possible manual energy as well as the least needed, "will-to-write" energy, since it seemed to me that any need for the invoking of THOSE energies would interfere with and deflect the more elusive "thought and impression" energy whose shape and gesture I hope to *trap* upon the page.

But the writing technique does not end with that certain crest of thought washing itself lightly onto the page where it leaves its idiosyncratic trace. Since the physical "writing" is but part of a larger cycle of "being in life" in a certain way—every element of that cycle interacting, mixing, and altering the terms of the other elements—it is important to realize that the following stages are stages of the "writing" itself, and though they occur "later in time," the pen-on-page writing is always molding itself to the already-existing contours of those later movements which include: 1) the physical act of typing the handwritten manuscript 2) the various problem-solving moments of staging 3) my own experiencing of audience-watching-the-play, which involves my own adjustments of the rhythm of performance, which I control from the sound booth during each performance. (Though this last aspect may change this year, as I plan to present the first Ontological-Hysteric Theater production for which I will not be operating the sound.)

1) To type the handwritten text, which had included illustrations and graphological variations of all sorts, is to eliminate certain wideness of texture which, in the original manuscript, represents for me a very special "wideness" of mental posture. The text as handwritten is the making of a concrete, physical object. Writing as the encrustation of a history of "marking"—of INSCRIBING mind into matter. To type is to transform this "archeological record" into a digital, bodyless form which only the staging will return to concrete, physical reality. The idiosyncrasies of handwriting and sketch will reemerge in the staging—in a different form, which may make the "meaning" of the original text drift a bit. That mediating "typed" text is an important step which takes away from the original fullness, so that a void of sorts is created, which will then evoke the necessary "filling" action of the staging. The resultant "drift" is also important to me, as it opens the text and the original impulses to a degree of contingency and improvisation which can only testify to the integral "truth" (i.e. inhabitableness) of the process I have set in motion, which reveals one aspect of itself under the guise of "text" (or, if you will, play).

2) I have indicated that the staging is a series of problem-solving tasks which "re-concretizes" the text. It's a matter of finding equivalencies for the densities and special "auras" established by the graphics—typographic as well as drawn— of the original manuscript. The sound-layering I use—tapes of repeated words, noises, music—also serves to reflect the multiple pulls of the visual and ideational aspects of man-

uscript. As you can see, the staging, then, is not an attempt to CONVINCE the audience of the play's reality or verisimilitude . . . but rather an effort to rewrite the text back into manuscript (the imprint of the personal hand) style.

3) Finally, the audience comes, and I am in front of my text, and they are watching me watch my text. And the performance is segmented by noises and tape cues which I control—and just as the text's generation is an attempt to re-segment the ordinary flow of my life by establishing a new balance between moments when the hand is moving over the paper and moments when it is not—so that segmentation in performance is both a reflection of and a continuation of that approach to writing as resegmentation. It is a CONTINUATION of my writing process.

I should add at this point, that the text-making process I have described, which skims the crest off the wave of my living (and to which I then try to retune my living, out of which will emerge the next crest of writing), that process continues over the days and weeks and does not stop and begin for each "play" but is a continual process from which "plays" are later extracted. At a certain point I pick up one of my notebooks, look casually through it and decide "Hum . . . go from here to here and I have a play," which means that the text of any given work is a series of "change of subjects"—which I believe becomes the subject of the work itself as the continual change-of-subject, interruption, re-beginning, reflects the true shape and texture of conscious experience, which recognized and reflected in the work of art puts us in the very "place" where being-human becomes a free and creative way-of-being. (An extended meditation on this subject of play-of-changes-of-subject will be included in the program for my next production this winter.)

Suffice it to say at this point that when I said, at the beginning of this article, that my plays were "about" HOW I WRITE, I meant that the writing is generated in a certain way which ends up producing structures with a form and texture which is the very embodiment of the theories and goals which are the "reasons for doing the writing." And it happened because at a certain point in my life I became convinced that the more one tried to write a play "about" some subject, the more one invariably lied about that subject, left out the very way in which that subject manifested itself in the real life of real people—the more one simply alluded very vaguely to "something not present" in the writing itself. And I began, instead, to attempt to radicalize and illuminate the true processes and tendencies within my own "living and doing"—which happened to be my writing of plays. While the deepest, most serious and pertinent "subject" of the work is always this "method of making the process be—in the way of embodying itself" establishing thereby a BEACON by which other parts of life can be charted, it is equally true that the human tendency to converge toward certain institutionalized "shapes" of more ordinary and schematized meaning-patterns can hardly be avoided, and I have discovered that in staging each of my plays, more conventional "themes" always emerge—but they are, to me, not central, not the source of energy and illumination after which I quest. (For the doubters, I will simply state that, for instance, *Pandering to the Masses* clearly centered itself on this second more superficial level on the relation between knowing and dying to habit and convention; *Rhoda in Potatoland* on the physicality and urge to tumescence of all "body-things" as they try to swamp mind-things in us; *Book of Splendors* on the world experienced as pure "multiplicity" and the mind's effort to steer clearly through, and using, that multiplicity.)

How I write my plays? I try to let them grow, in the fields and oceans of my days which succeed one another, each day reattacking the *same* problem with that "change of subject" that is the new day. So I try to write in such a way that the mark on the page is NOT a continuation, but a change of direction, always a change of direction, always something that was till now "left out" . . . only to find out in the end that it WAS a continuation after all. My habit is to try and write BEFORE writing, to make the writing the preparation BEFORE writing. Pen always in hand, paper ready to catch its scribble . . . "Humm . . . I *MIGHT* write such and such . . ." And through that "I *MIGHT*" (which I think of as somewhat akin to the Brechtian acting technique of "showing," of commenting upon the gesture "as-if" it were really being made), through such an "I *MIGHT*" of writing, the rest of the world of the not-written is still somehow available, and the writing (and reading and seeing it staged) is a training in a certain psychic posture of keeping all alternatives and departures from THAT moment and THAT impulse available. To "MIGHT write" is to stay in the center of where writing arises. Where thinking arises. Where living arises. Only it's not a center . . . it's an everywhere.

SEVEN ADDITIONAL INTERESTING IDEAS
WHICH ARE NOT IN THE ABOVE ARTICLE,
BUT NOW THEY ARE

(You see? The article turns into something more like one of my plays, and you see how they get written.)

First—why are these ideas not "in" the article? Because the article is "trying to write an article," and that means automatically that things that don't fit in the article might get left out but still might be important things. Even more important—they might have been left out of the article because of a certain FAILURE of a certain sort on my part, but that FAILURE of a certain sort might lead to the following NEW idea, which is having a list of interesting different things at the end of the article, and that might be more interesting than a fully integrated and whole article because it implies and embodies the underlying and exciting conflict going on in the writing: the conflict between the energy of being-in-a-certain-stream of stylistic discourse, and the energy of having certain ideas I wanted to express BEFORE I had entered and been absorbed by that discursive stream. That conflict between "expression," the self-energizing environment it creates around the writer vs. the claims of ideas, insights or images he—outside of being-in-the-writing—wishes to communicate . . . that conflict is basic and echoed in many life fields other than "writing plays."

But here are the seven ideas (and the decision to have just seven was arrived at PREVIOUS to formulating for myself exactly what those ideas would be). I thought to myself, "Ah, this article seems a bit short, so perhaps seven more items . . ." (Why did I think it short? What relevance did its length have to what I anticipated and hoped might be its effect upon the readers of this magazine?) All these considerations, all these grounds for making decisions about the form and style of this article seem to me reflected in the shape of the article and, therefore, the article EMBODIES its ideas as well as speaks about them—which is (I think) what my plays do.

> 1) Sleep. I take naps during the day. To "clear" my mind, so that I can "begin again"—start a new day, as it were, whose writing will come from a new place. It's as if my writing were trying to define some "unseeable" object whose outline can only be traced through a one-step-removed method akin to the physicist's method of firing electrons at a particle and catching the electron's patterns of deflection on a photographic plate. So I "fire" bursts of writing

at an invisible particle (a certain state of being, a certain dreamed-of intuited level of consciousness or attention) and the writing, some of it, hits the page. But then, to avoid being dragged into the river of that "discourse which has just gotten under way," I need to move back to the firing area. I SLEEP, I NEGATE THE DRIFT of the writing burst I've just fired, its tendency to live its own life and write its own development. I wake up cleansed, and fire again!

2) John Gassner, my teacher at Yale, used to greet his playwright students when meeting casually in the street or corridor with, "Hello, hello, well how is the scribbling going?" Though I'm sure it was far from what he had in mind—my habit is to radicalize that suggestion of his and make my handwriting large, sloppy, like a scribble, so that things besides intention come through. At least, another level of intention. Sometimes, when I then come to type up the manuscript, there are words I cannot make out. Yet they must be typed—so something from another place within me is allowed, at that point, to interfere. In addition, in the handwritten manuscript, I no longer indicate who is saying what line—the *field* is doing the speaking. Usually the lines are not assigned until rehearsal—and even in performance I want to keep that feeling of a primordial "scribble" out of which discourse and meaning slowly built their empire.

3) My habit is, when in writing a unit of six or seven lines, I come to a halt (and even from the beginning, when I was in school, writing "realistic" plays, I would compose one to six lines at a time, then wander about for ten minutes, then a few more, etc.), often to "shock" the writing back into alertness I will shift the grammatic "person" reference in order to angle the active-in-the-scene perspective differently. It's a bit, I suppose, like a cut in the movies. In other words, Rhoda is saying things referring to herself in the normal first person, and then she will suddenly shift to self-reference in the third person. The point is this shift is not to imply something about HER psychology or aim within the scene, but is an articulating of the writing itself—I wish to (need to, in order to have the energy to go on writing!) shift the parameters of the scene or unit. Then, of course, the further things being said will somehow have to reflect upon or embody the implications of that shift.

4) My reading. Which goes on in snatches during the writing. Shifts, skips, makes a collage of reading so that the reading seems often to be a means of orientation which will keep me (my head) EQUIDISTANT from a variety of tendencies of thought and feeling. In other words, my "writing-habit" of reading is to use the reading as a tuning mechanism—NOT to be tuned to what I am reading, but to keep myself "widened" and available (to what is not present). To make all the "readings"—in collaboration with what else is happening in the space where I am—keep me from being in a "center," which would deny, for the moment, the reality of things in OTHER centers.

5) I can't WILL the changes of subject of which my work is made. Sometimes I try to—I think, "OK, that scene seems good and enough of that, now I want to start from another place in such a way that the reverberations between the two will be productive . . ." and I make the attempt to "begin-again," but it never works. I have to wait for the next day, or go to sleep, or hope that I will be "distracted" and then, not willed, something else gets scribbled on the page and, having forgotten the context of surrounding pages, the new item is the one I've been waiting for and produces the proper reverberations. (Again, when I come to select my twenty or thirty pages of manuscript for staging, I must insist that I am always moved by the way in which the unifying context of the new play slowly emerges, the same and yet a different perspective upon that "same" for each different play.)

6) My habit is, sometimes, to see a unit I've just written, find it just TOO terrible or simplistic or flat or embarrassing or badly written . . . and cross it out. Then, if that crossed-out section happens to fall within those pages I've chosen to stage, I end up feeling guilty about trying to "cast-off" something which did indeed come out of me, no matter how much it embarrassed me, and I decide to stage that crossed-out section along with the rest. Needless to say, in the finished product, that crossed-out section usually proves to be one of the stronger and more memorable moments of the piece.

7) It is my habit to prepare and refine my theoretical approach to my art with a never-ending stream of notes and observations, which pile up on loose pages placed next to my typewriter or tacked to a bulletin board, and that activity accompanies on most days the growth of a play-text material proper; and often, having written out for myself a theoretical excerpt I will then directly provide myself with a little illustration of the notion, and that illustration is part of the play-text later on, when that text is selected. But I have not the slightest hesitation at any point to a) directly contradict any of my theoretical notes in any way whatsoever that comes to me, and b) accept and include anything that comes to me arbitrarily for any reason from any source—so long as the hand with pen is twitching and lets that material onto the page. And yet the resultant work (whether one likes it or does not like it) is clearly consistent, whole, and possessed of a certain mysterious logic which will one day explain itself more fully.

8) (Which is one more than was promised.) It is my habit to end my plays abruptly, but with a certain ambiguity as to whether or not the play is indeed over. That kind of "ending" happens many times in my work previous to the ending. And it always happens in my head, which is always "changing the subject"—but in a certain way.

TWO INTERVIEWS

AN INTERVIEW WITH RICHARD FOREMAN

by Julia Lee Barclay

September 25, 2008

JLB: So my first question is quite simple: what is your experience with philosophy in general, and do you see a relationship between philosophy and your own work?

RF: My introduction to philosophy was in college. In my sophomore year I took a course from a man who was a student of Ortega's [Ortega y Gasset]. Ortega is out of favor these days as a reactionary philosopher, but I went home that summer and read Ortega. I hadn't really read any philosophy before that, and I was knocked out. I remember sitting on the lawn and reading a couple of sentences and just going haaahhh, sitting back and letting what I had just read rattle inside of me for a minute or so. Later on, after I graduated from college—where I felt, aside from that course, that I was taught very little that was of any use, and very little that was accurate—I started reading a lot of different philosophers, religious writers, psychoanalysts, people writing on aesthetics. That was my main preoccupation—reading that stuff. And at a certain point, after having a slightly mystical experience, I started to write a different kind of play. I wanted the experience of watching a play to have something to do with the reading experience—to get the same kind of kick from watching the aesthetic moves, these little epiphanies of the play. It was the same aesthetic kick that I got from reading a dense text that would continually flip me around and reintroduce me to seeing the world in a different way. That's what I get from philosophy—seeing what's around you and realizing that it operates rather differently than you thought. To me, that's a tremendous moment of aesthetic pleasure and it's what I think I'm after in my work.

Would you be willing to talk about the mystical experience you had?

Oh, sure. I've talked about it many times. My mystical experience— and I don't claim it's special—was when I threw myself down on the bed once in frustration and the moment I hit the bed it was as if my head turned into a globe that was about six feet in diameter. Everything inside of me was on this transparent globe and everything in the outside world was in this transparent globe. They were in the same place, everything was there at once, and it was all perfect, it was just ecstatic. I felt that way for maybe twenty minutes, which is a long time for an experience like that, and then it gradually faded. But that didn't directly influence what I was writing. The experience that changed the way I was writing was later. One day after graduating from the Yale Drama School, where I was trying to write plays like Arthur Miller or Brecht or whoever, I remember pulling myself back from the table and saying, "You know, this is ridiculous. If you walk into a theater tonight, what would you really like to see happening?" And I had this vision of two performers looking at each other across the stage with a certain kind of tension and nothing else happening, and I started at that moment writing a very different kind of play, which is vaguely akin to what I've been doing ever since.

It sounds like there's a relationship between the experience you had with texts that shift points of view and the mystical experience that shifted your point of view. When you're working do you try to make that shift happen?

I find it's not useful. I always try to be open and I never work in terms of a schematic. I always try to blank out and put down what comes. I accept what comes. In the early days I had the Kerouac rule—whatever comes, don't interfere, you're not allowed to rewrite—then after ten years I started rewriting and now I rewrite like crazy. I rewrite everything. I don't know ahead of time where I'm going but as I rework the material I do tend to shape it. First it's like the patient in analysis and then the analyst takes over and tries to shape the material.

Directing is different. I've always wanted to be that open in my directing but I find it very difficult. Faced with these people who expect me to do something, a more reactionary self takes over. I have to be in charge, to show people I know what I'm doing, and I find it very difficult to just sit there and let anything happen because I'm not particularly interested in what the actors will invent. I find it's never relevant to what I'm trying to do.

Now, it's different since I've started working with film. I'm on the verge of maybe giving up theater completely and just working on film. I may not be as good at it but I don't care. In working in film, I discovered that I just want to watch. I gather material very quickly, I shoot very quickly and then I edit for months. I'm just trying to watch and see what grows out of what I have, so it is evoking a different part of me to work in this other medium, with different philosophical implications. Lately I keep trying to tell myself I don't want to do something to impress people or have an effect on anybody. I don't believe in any of that anymore. I always maintained that I was making art for myself and offering it for others who needed it. I was not ever trying to achieve a certain effect on the audience, but I was always trying to make great, solid, significant art, whatever that means. I'm trying to free myself from that. I doubt that I'll succeed but I want to be more Zen-like and work the way certain European filmmakers work—staying open to what comes to them and letting the camera capture it.

Have any of these shifts in your work come from a philosophy you've read, or is it purely intuitive?

I'm always reading philosophers to see if what they're saying relates to what I'm doing. That's mostly the kick I've gotten from reading philosophy for the last twenty years—that it justifies what I'm doing. Perhaps it's because of my upbringing as a nice upper-middle-class Jewish boy whose parents always said, "Why are you doing this crazy stuff?" I think the reason I read philosophy was to try to find people who would reassure me that I wasn't wasting my time—and they did, mammothly. They convinced me that what I was doing was right.

So you were using philosophy in a retrospective way?

Yes and no. I take notes all the time. I have piles of theoretical notes, where I'll be reading somebody and he'll say, "Art should be blah blah blah," and I'll write that in the margin of the book, and later on

I might type it up so it feeds into me. But mostly it feeds into the huge stack of notes that will eventually give me the system that I can use to write the next play. But of course when it comes time to write the next play, I never pay them any attention.

Do you find that you read contradictory philosophies? Because there's a lot of arguing going on in your work.

I don't think about it in those terms. I remember Wittgenstein saying that he doesn't read books, he just looks through them for hints, and I'm looking for hints. So they may be contradictory if you place them in the context of the whole system, but they're not contradictory in terms of my choices.

But when I see your work one of the things I like about it is that it seems as though you're arguing with yourself.

Oh no, it's less argument and more saying, "Life is such and such, but you take that seriously?" It's trying to indicate ironically that it's just anything that is said, the selection of one out of a million different perspectives, and in the end they are all equally relevant.

Is that one of the reasons you're trying to get out of Great Art mode?

Yeah, but not consciously. And I'm having difficulty. I've been drifting that way for many years but I always get pulled back because I have been conditioned by another kind of psychological upbringing, a psychological orientation that I've always been trying to escape but I suspect I never will.

Do you really want to?

Maybe not, I don't know. The pole that the alternative way provides keeps me going in a way.

I'm sorry, which is the alternative?

The alternative is the more open, neutral way, like [Roland] Barthes's book, *The Neutral*, which talks about the whiteness of things, the blankness of things and the neutrality of things as the source of great psychic energy. But all those other people, the ones that everybody always talks about —

The French men?

Yeah, and there are some German guys. There are even a few Americans!

I know you're not into [Jacques] Lacan right now, but when you wrote in Unbalancing Acts about being a dumb reader of Lacan, it seemed like you were writing about the difficulty you had with it.

I said that, but it may or may not be true. I've read a ton of Lacan, a lot of secondary stuff. I have a whole bookcase full of books on Lacan. But again, I'm looking for hints, and I've never felt guilty about skimming through books until something catches my eye and marking that, and sometimes getting caught and reading a little more densely.

At a certain point the whole French notion (which is not in Lacan) that we are born into this language that imprisons us and we are broken people, was very important to me. I have no doubt that Lacan's difficult style was part of his appeal because I like the riddle or the enigma or the oracle because it frees you to get that first lightning flash. I always refer back to Alain, I think it was, and the notion that it's not good for an artist to develop things. I try not to develop things because the minute you start developing things you get trapped in the system. So I read these people not to get a handle on their whole system. Occasionally there's been somebody that I've thought, "Well, I've really got to study and understand what so and so is talking about," but usually not.

Can you give an example of one?

I can give an example but it won't make my standing seem too high in the philosophy world. When I was coming out of college I discovered [George] Gurdjieff. I remember reading everything and also reading through a lot of other sources and trying to understand his system. I read a lot of secondary Lacan to try to understand his system also. So I suppose it's debatable if he's a philosopher but of course it's also debatable whether Gurdjieff is a philosopher.

Can you tell me how either Lacan or Gurdjieff might have altered your writing or your rehearsal style?

No, not particularly. It had an effect on me, on the person who was then writing out of blankness and waiting to see what came. I hate art where I see somebody try to embody what this thinker has to say. I have no interest in that. I know some people who do that and I don't like their work.

With Bad Boy Nietzsche! were you interested in something specific with his philosophy, or was it looking at him as a person?

I worked the same way. The only thing I used directly from Nietzsche were certain poetic fragments from *The Gay Science*. I just operated out of the the image of him throwing his arms around the horse in Torino and the things that came easily from whatever knowledge I had of Nietzsche. So I was very, very proud of the fact that at the end of the year *Art Forum* asked these people to comment on ten events of the year and Arthur Danto said *Bad Boy Nietzsche!* was great and it felt just like Nietzsche. But again, I certainly did not work schematically and say, "How can I express for people what Nietzsche had to say?" I just knew Nietzsche slightly and let it lead my imagination.

Why Nietzsche rather than, say, Bad Boy Lacan?

[laughter] That's a dumb question.

[laughter] I know, but I'm asking you anyway.

At one point I thought it was going to be about Nietzsche and Rimbaud and that didn't work. So I don't know. It just came to me. Nietzsche is one of those people who's better at the center. I wouldn't use Lacan because he's not available enough to everybody as a frame of reference. Not that people know what Nietzsche really said or who he really was, but still, you say, "Nietzsche," and everyone will say, "Oh yeah, Nietzsche."

Right, so it has this strange—

Resonance.

So do you think of theater and film in any way as philosophy itself, or as a metaphor for it?

I've been thinking lately that what is most valuable to me about making art is less the work of art itself than the fact that struggling with it forces me to have all kinds of thoughts that I would not otherwise have. It stimulates a kind of mental process in trying to come to terms with it. Perhaps that's the most interesting aspect of it for me, because when I'm writing, or when I'm editing, I'm still continually reading and getting new ideas, and in a way I find that more interesting than having produced a finished work. I certainly don't claim that I'm doing philosophy, though what I'm doing is trying to make an object that reflects the truth in some way as I experience it. So I guess in a sense that's philosophy.

When you're making decisions in rehearsal, when you're asking people to shift positions or whatever, is there any conscious thing going on or are you working off complete intuition?

Does complete intuition make it look more right, more interesting and less stupid, less obvious? I think it's like a painter. Picasso doesn't think, "I would better express the anguish of life if I changed that from orange to green." No, you just blank out and do what something is telling you to do.

You talk a lot about the writing process. Do you find any of that same stimulation when you're working with actors?

No, I don't like working with the actors much. I like them. Some are very talented. I'm not putting them down, but they don't interest me much. Occasionally I work with somebody where I sit back and go, "Wow, whatever you're doing, do it." But it's different because it's a process of social interchange. I tend to be a hermit and one of the reasons I've stayed in theater is that it has forced me to deal with people because I don't want to dry up. But many years ago I stopped working with designers because I discovered that having to go through the verbal mechanism and deal with another person just isn't the same. There's not the same degree of creativity or discovery as when you're alone making your model, allowing yourself to be sloppy or stupid in ways you can't be when you're interacting with somebody else. In rehearsal I can't be as stupid and as sloppy as I can be when I'm writing. Now I may rewrite it and correct it, but the impulse that is producing it is different than what happens when you're working with a group of people and having to talk to them and communicate with them.

And with film that's different?

Yeah. I film very fast and I accept a lot of mistakes and invent things on the spot. Like this feature film I'm working on now, which is my first, I filmed it in three days and I've been editing for five months, eight or ten hours a day.

So the relationship you would be having with actors you're having with the film itself?

Like with writing or designing or painting, you can try anything. With filmmaking more than writing there are certain things that you have to force yourself to rethink. You know, "I worked so hard building this scene and making these edits, that's the way it's supposed to be." And it's terrible for an artist to feel "that's the way it's supposed to be."

Do you have the same problem of changing something when you're working with people onstage?

A little, but I'm ruthless. People are always shocked that I'll come in one day and cut my favorite scene because it's terrible.

How would you describe that moment when you look at something and decide either it's terrible or it's working?

The moment that seemed to work and all of a sudden it's stupid?

Right, what constitutes something stupid?

Something obvious, banal, too one-dimensional.

And on the opposite side, what constitutes something that works?

It's really dense, really tricky and hard to get your head around, but very clear.

And if you put enough of those together, then I assume your hope is that people will have that sense of rearrangement you were talking about?

I don't know if they can. I really don't do it for them. Obviously another part of me wants everybody in the world to think I'm a great artist, but I don't do anything to try and say, "Will people like this?" I have to fight that at all times.

It's hard to have both of those things at the same time, to both want people to like you and then not do anything—

It's a continual internal struggle. There are artists who care less than I do because of their upbringing and so forth, but it's hard for me to remember to reject that desire to please.

So you actively try to intervene with that then?

Oh, yes, when I notice it's happening.

And how does that work?

Well, I notice I'm thinking, "Oh, that's pretty effective," and I'm really thinking unconsciously, "Wow, that'll get 'em, that'll please 'em."

So it's like another part of you comes in and does the editing for you?

A lot of people that work with me always think I'm throwing out so many things that people would really love. I'm not sure they would, but they think so and maybe that's one of the reasons I'm throwing some of them out.

Do you think there's any philosophy that made you have the impulse of trying not to please?

I've spent my whole life doing things that most people don't like, things I didn't like at first and then came to realize were great. But I've got to say that in the back of my mind I suspect that I am trying to please one or two super-sensitive, intelligent people. I think most audiences are dumb, and I can also be dumb. Last year we would have a talk-back one night a week where I would talk to the audience, and I've gotta admit that often the audience would be coming in and I'd say to the ticket guy, "Wow, they look like clods tonight. Where did these people come from?" And then in the talk-back it turned out they were very bright. But I do have a prejudice.

I remember I asked you a question once, ages ago, in the mid-nineties. I was sitting in the audience and I was the only person laughing and people were staring at me. I said to you, "It is supposed to be funny, isn't it?" and you said yes.

I think I'm basically a comic artist.

It's very interesting the way humor gets used. I find that when people feel they are in an intellectual environment there is a fear of seeming wrong by having fun or laughing in any way.

All of my life I've been interested in these people and I must admit on the few occasions when I've been to conferences and people are talking about Lacan or whatever I've gone out of my skull with bore-dom it's so stodgy.

This is why I'm talking to artists who read philosophy, because I don't know if you've ever been to a conference and heard a philosophical paper about laughter but it's one of the most unfunny things you can ever do.

Philosophers are just like everybody else. I think everything could be cut by at least three quarters—it's always too long. It's the same thing with art and philosophy, I mean really.

Well, speaking of that, I'll let you go. Is there anything else you'd like to say about art and philosophy in general?

Everybody always asks that. I just say things in response to what people want to hear. I don't have anything to say, really. I've always dreamed of being someone who didn't have anything to say, who wouldn't talk, and I've always mistrusted what I say. Am I really speaking the truth or am I just trying to impress people, trying to impress myself?

But you put that in the work, don't you?

I try to.

My experience of watching your work is that I go into it with one brain and come out with another, which is a lovely experience and very rare.

I know, it is. My particular bugaboo is Ingmar Bergman, because I always thought that his films, which I really hated, were just everybody inflating their chests and saying, "We are serious upper-middle-class sophisticated people with great sexual and spiritual problems and that's what makes us important and interesting, especially our emotional and sexual problems." I find it so phony. I don't want to be like that.

Is there anything in your upbringing or that you read where you can locate when that started?

I think it's from coming from an upper-middle-class Jewish fam-ily. My parents weren't intellectuals at all, but they encouraged me to be interested in art. They still would laugh at modern paintings and my father would say, "I could do that," but they would take me to the museums. There was still that Jewish culture. So I think it comes from Jewishness. I mean, look at Woody Allen, who I don't particularly like, but there is a tradition of not taking yourself too seriously.

A lot of people think of your work as cerebral, but I actually find it emotional.

Absolutely, I think it's very emotional. The thing I think about is feeling. Feeling can be emotional and it can also be intellectual. But it's feeling, colors, sadness. There's a lot of sadness in my work. It's elegiac, realizing death is coming. You know, death is coming to me soon and that is certainly informing my work.

Somehow it always has, though.

It has.

That's why the humor is there.

Yes, absolutely.

AN INTERVIEW WITH RICHARD FOREMAN

by Morgan von Prelle Pecelli

October 12, 2009/December 2, 2009

MP: We're here to talk about metaphysics, but I wonder if maybe I ought to start with a question that Ken Jordan asked you almost twenty years ago, when he was interviewing you for *Unbalancing Acts*. Ken was asking you about an underlying interest in a basic spiritual grounding, implying that you were clearing away a lot of dramatic and excess acting. Is that still true?

RF: Well, that's always been the case, though I think the word "spiritual" is a bit pretentious and a little fuzzy. I've always been concerned with—and I am now to an even more radical degree—seeing daily life and daily behavior as a prison that we can't escape, a total façade that is meaningless, but that we can't deny. It's there. So the task is to use art to erase the surface—not to get to depth, because I'm not sure I believe in any further depth—but to erase the surface so you can really watch.

You see, it's a difficult time to talk to me because I'm making this transition from theater to film, and at the moment I'm deeply immersed in finishing this play, so I'm sort of confused because I'm back to thinking about certain problems in the theater, which basically are problems that no longer interest me, and all of my focus is on seeing rather than doing. The theater, however, is not about seeing. The theater is about doing, about making things happen. And I find that, at least in terms of my own life, rather regressive.

The doing.

Yeah, the doing—moving everything around, making things, making things happen. So I'm in a bit of a quandary at this point because that's where my head is until the play opens. My head is still trying to solve the problems of the play, but I've been solving them for forty years, and I'm interested in something else now.

Where does the film take you, where does the seeing take you? And, how is it different from the doing?

That's very hard to answer. I have tons of pages I've written about that. But I think one hardly has to say more than everything is the same, that it doesn't matter what you have, which is part and parcel of the way that I work in film. The way I work in film is that I shoot very fast, in three or four days. I get like twelve or fourteen setups. And I keep all kinds of mistakes. I keep giving instructions to the performers. Mistakes come in. These tableaus where people talk a little bit, do a few movements. I take this as raw material, and there isn't much thought, really. I work over it, edit it and edit it, for about a year. But that is just a deepening of the seeing, as far as I'm concerned. It's trying to see what is really there.

Because the tendency is to first look at a six-minute bit of material and your first reaction is, "Oh, that's interesting. That's dramatic. Oh, I could keep that." Or, "That's not very good." And you have to keep looking and looking and looking, until you see that all the things that were embarrassing or not very good—even if you edit them, even if you change the exposure—are still things to be looked at, are of just as much value as the things that seem more engaging.

Most film tries to draw you in and engage you, and I don't want to do that. I have no interest in that. I want to make you feel that the film is watching you, rather than you entering the film. The film is full of people staring at the camera and filling your space, much like Russian or Eastern European icons, which I've always been interested in.

You've used those for your posters.

No, those weren't icons. Those were from a seventeenth century French architect who was a schizophrenic, a great visionary architect who also made these strange pictures, these strange people.

But we had some of these icons. Kate [artist and actor Kate Manheim, Foreman's wife] was always interested in them. We bought each other icons for gifts and it's just the staring, the looking at you the icon does. What is the icon looking at? How is it entering your space? Well, there are whole philosophical analyses of those possibilities.

There's a Lacanian analysis of the object.

Yes. I remember Lacan saying of the fisherman, "Oh, you're looking at the tin can floating in the water. Don't you realize the tin can is looking at you?"

Are you playing with that at all?

Lately I have been thinking less about Lacan, though he dominated a lot of my thinking for probably fifteen years. But for the last five or six years, as I've told everybody, I've been continually reading and rereading this book, *Reality* by a man by the name of Peter Kingsley, who used to be a serious professor of pre-Socratic Greek philosophy and wrote one of the classic books in the field. And he's now even more serious because he went off the deep end and wrote a different kind of book, about how Parmenides and Empedocles, who are theoretically the founders of the Western rational tradition, were really magicians, that they were really shamans. He says they were really rooting the West in a kind of magical manipulation, which Plato and other people couldn't deal with and translated it into inventing logic—so people would have something to do with their minds, as he describes it.

It's like, give a dog a ball because he wants to be chewing, and the ball keeps him busy. Now, rationality and Western philosophy keeps us busy because we can't face up to the stillness, i.e., the watching that Parmenides placed at the root of Western philosophy. Everybody thinks he was talking about logic, which is a term he used, but it was a different thing.

Was he talking about logic or was he talking about the Platonic "Real"—that symbolic "Real" of the conceptual world as opposed to the lowercase, material reality?

No, mostly he's talking about how everything is deception. We live in a world of total deception, and we have to be very tricky to move within that deception. Accept it. Let ourselves be deceived. Know that we are being deceived. And know how to navigate that, to experience the stillness behind it. Now he doesn't talk about watching, but I translate it into relating to the kind of watching that I find myself doing as I'm working on film, as opposed to what was happening when I was working on theater.

When you are working on film, you said that you are trying to get it so that the audience feels they are being watched, but also there's a "watching of the Real." Was the "doing of the Real" happening in your theater?

I don't know because this is after the fact. This is when I try to figure out for myself why the hell I'm doing this instead of writing a play like David Mamet. And these things that I read seem to relate to it. But when I'm actually making the art I'm just blanking out and saying, "What do I really want?" And the interesting thing is that in making film and having people look into the camera, and then doing this watching, I'm really returning to the kind of theater I made back in the late sixties, when everybody used to walk out of my plays because they thought they were too boring.

Like *Angelface* and *Rhoda In Potatoland (Her Fall-Starts)*?

Yeah. Those plays were all about actors just standing there, looking at the audience, long pauses, a little bit of movement, very basic things being said, and the whole moment of the play was as if to say to the audience, "OK, here's a statement. What do you make of this? Here's a body, audience. What are you going to do with this?" And really now, towards the end of my life, in making films I'm returning to that style. Now, there are big differences, but there's a return to that.

Back in the sixties and seventies, when everybody was walking out of your shows, there was a certain amount of freedom that you had to explore those things. Do you feel that you're in a similar position now, at the beginning of this film work?

Oh, absolutely. And though I was not making films then, my friends were the underground filmmaking community around Jonas Mekas. And those people liked what I did. So if everybody walked out of my play, there were a couple of them that didn't. And I felt, well, these are the only people that count. And as I started making films, I said to everybody, "You know, I'm so sick of this theater, and worrying about people, worrying about how they respond. Even though I work for myself, I'm still hurt when people don't like it." So I thought,

"Why don't I make films for the next ten years, and I'll put an ad in the *Voice*, if anybody still reads the *Voice*, and it will say: 'Richard Foreman is now making films, and they will be viewable on the day of his death.'" It's not what I'm going to do, but it's a pretty good idea. Because I am certainly nauseated by this whole idea of pushing my stuff out into the public.

It would also free you from any response whatsoever from anybody else, and therefore would free you to make whatever you wanted.

But in a sense that's what I've tried to do for years. Of course, one of the many selves within me, in a Gurdjieffian sense, cares about what people say, even though I've always made things thinking only what keeps me interested, what keeps me awake. But you know, I don't believe that even Neil Simon thinks about the audience *all* the time. Maybe he does, I don't know. It's hard for me to believe that any artist doesn't basically make what is going to give him delight.

I've been very lucky, because I've been mostly working through my own theater. But normally in the theater, there are all kinds of people who come and offer their opinions, and you have to listen to them. They are giving you the money. They are the producers, and the producer's wife. And many people say that's the glory of the theater. It's the collective thing. It's not just you. But I don't have any interest in collectives.

Of course, a painter doesn't operate that way. I don't think Picasso was painting and saying as he painted, "Would you come and tell me what color I should put here?" No, that's nonsense. I don't think that's the way an artist functions. And for that reason, I don't think that theater is art. And normally that's also the way film functions, but it was not the way the underground filmmakers functioned. That's why back when I was starting to make my theater I was only seeing underground film and I thought I was seeing some sort of presentational art form that made sense to me. It seemed pure and ravishing and wonderful to me.

If theater isn't art, what is it?

Entertainment. It's part of the entertainment industry.

You've said before that with the pieces that you're making you're trying to fill a gap, something that's missing in the world.

Well, missing in my life. Yeah.

Can you talk a little bit about that?

What's missing in my life? Well, start with the whole socialization process. Like I have to talk to you now. I have to present myself in a certain way. And, like everybody else, I've been conditioned that there are certain things I wouldn't do. You know, I wouldn't— [RF makes faces while vocalizing incomprehensible sounds]. There are all kinds of behavior I wouldn't allow to surface. And I'm not saying that it surfaces when I'm alone in my room and nobody else is there. But we exist in terms of categories that are imposed upon us by society and our upbringing. And I think that cuts off a lot of impulses.

I mean why do people think that kids are so great? Because they haven't been socialized yet. Kids are still operating out of impulses. And people say that you can't have a society that way. But why do artists exist? I think even if they train and discipline themselves, they are still trying to be responsive to certain impulses, to certain abilities, to see, even impulsively, what in most people has been schooled out.

Through disciplinary practices?

Well, some disciplinary practices do serve artists. But no, through social practices that each society deems OK. In other words, why do different societies come up with different painting styles? It's hard to say exactly where they come from. But obviously, if you're in Persia in the seventeenth century you paint differently than you paint in New York today. Why? Well, because you are in a milieu that keeps certain channels open and other channels closed off.

Is this where your suspicion of the collective comes from?

Oh, yes, but it comes from everywhere. Even as a little kid, I hated collective stuff. It could be because I'm adopted and my mother did not breast feed me. [laughs] Maybe it has something to do with that. But I always rejected the American need to be friendly. It makes me nauseous. I mean, I am the kind of the person that hated singing in a chorus. I couldn't hear myself so I didn't know what the hell I was doing. It was no good.

Most people know the film that Leni Riefenstahl made about Hitler's Nuremberg rally called *Triumph of the Will*. It's all these Nazis marching up and down with great spotlights and big spectacle, and everybody says, "Well, the Nazis were terrible, but you've got to admit that film about the Nuremberg rally is pretty wonderful." I never got that. To me, it looks like a lot of my old gym teachers, slightly pudgy middle-aged men who are trying to act tough, dressing up in funny costumes and marching along. I don't get it.

But maybe that's from my upbringing and my early situation. And that's what everybody has to deal with, but the problem is most people are not in a situation where they can openly and honestly deal with the idiosyncratic nature of their being placed in the world in a certain way and therefore having a certain perspective. Instead, they learn to smooth that out, so it's more like the perspective of everybody else, so they can get along. And that's horrible.

Is it a veil between us and Reality?

Yes, but of course you have to accept it. You mentioned Lacan earlier. Lacan, of course, identifies the "Real" as that which you cannot touch, which you cannot define, which evades our language and perceptual systems. So yes, it's a veil between you and Reality, but you aren't going to make contact with Reality no matter what you do.

Your theater is called the Ontological-Hysteric Theater. Is your film going to be Ontological-Hysteric Film? Is that moniker going to travel with you into this new medium?

I don't know. I'm not thinking about it. The only thing I know is I'm calling my first film *Richard Foreman Photo Play* [the final title was *Once Every Day*] because that's what films were originally called: photo plays. And that's what they are. There are theatrical elements, in its confrontational aspect, in its tableau aspect. It's just that I see all these films that people like and they are so disgusting to me.

You know, films are for people who are tired and want a little escape, and who want something to do on Saturday night. Art films aren't made anymore. There was that tradition, especially in European art films. But it's over. It's over.

Is film art or entertainment?

It depends what you do. There are certain films that are art. Some of the films of my friend Michael Snow are art. I think Béla Tarr films are art. Maybe some Godard and some Bresson are art. But it's very rare.

What about this theater piece that you're in the midst of making right now? It's with Willem Dafoe. You worked with Willem at The Performing Garage how many years ago?

Miss Universal Happiness. I would have to look up what year it was. Early eighties, mid-eighties.

Has a lot changed since you last worked together?

No, not really. He is extremely easy to work with. He's happy to be given a lot of instructions, a lot of ideas.

You said back then it was really nice to work with The Wooster Group because if you asked them to throw themselves against a wall, they would run and hurl themselves against a wall without question. There was something about that freedom that you found—

Yes, it's basically the same. But he's a big movie star. He's done a lot of things. I mean, sometimes he does wonder, "Richard, why are you saying this?" And then he says, "Oh, I never would have thought of that. OK, that's good."

You wrote this piece a while ago. And you've been rewriting it and reworking it. You've never staged it, though.

I wrote it about twelve years ago. And when I finished it there were certain things that really haunted me, but a lot of it didn't work. It seemed too obvious or corny. So I didn't stage it. But through the years, every once in a while I thought, "Maybe that *Idiot Savant* . . ." But I'd look at it again, and I'd have the same reaction.

Then a couple of years ago I called up Michael Gordon. I'd heard a record of Michael Gordon, a CD, and I just called him up. I didn't know him. I said, "I love your music. I'd like to do something with you." And we had a couple of ideas. And then I thought, "I could take certain elements of *Idiot Savant.* I'll sit down and rewrite them as if someone were singing." And, I gave it to him. There are two or three scenes that were in an opera we did at the REDCAT theater through CalArts. And then with Willem, after he left The Wooster Group, I'd see him in the streets. And I don't know how it came up. Maybe he said, "Why don't you direct me in a play?" So I had to think of something.

And I had this script. Another filmmaker that I respect very much is Portuguese filmmaker Manoel de Oliveira, who is now one hundred and he's still making films. And he worked on a lot of his best films with a writer who is probably in her late eighties or nineties. Agustina Bessa-Luis, who, though she has written a lot of novels, has never been translated into English. Which is a great tragedy. But I read somewhere she did a play called *Kierkegaard and Eroticism*. So I had a contact in Portugal and I said, "Can you get me this play, somehow?" She said, "I know Bessa-Luis. I'll try." Bessa-Luis sent me a rather rare copy of this script. I got a translator and he translated it. And I thought it was wonderful and that Willem would really be good playing Kierkegaard. I said, "Willem, I've got this script, but it's pretty esoteric. Why don't you take a look at it?" So he took a look at it and said, "Yeah, I could do that."

We soon realized it wasn't right for my theater and we couldn't find any theater that would take the risk of doing such a cerebral play. And I said, "Well, I have this other idea. I have this script that I've always thought about. Maybe if I rewrote *Idiot Savant*." So I rewrote it and it was still no good. I ended up rewriting it about ten times before I finally sent it to him. And he said, "Oh yeah, let's do this." And then I rewrote it a couple more times. So the basic kernel of each scene is the same but it's pretty well transformed. It's an old play that's a new play.

This is going to sound ridiculous, me asking you this question, but what is it about?

It is about the Idiot Savant, who is essentially making fun of every attempt to make sense of the world, and ends up embracing babble. Just, "blah, glah, gluh, glah." Essentially, it's not what you believe, it's what you do with whatever you choose to believe this week. So, that's what it's about.

And the film you're working on right now?

Well, the film is called, *Speaking for Dead People* [it was later abandoned]. And I filmed it with students at the most prestigious theater school in Germany, which is only for directors. Who knows— maybe people will hate it. I think it's pretty interesting, but it's very different from what people are used to looking at.

Are you going to start working with other footage?

Oh, yes. I have a lot of footage that hasn't been used in my plays. Because, as you know, for three years I was doing plays that had a continual one-hour filmed background that just ran through the whole play. And that was footage we shot in different countries. And now, I have a lot left to work with. I have Denmark, Zurich, Buffalo and Bucharest. I think I am going to work on the Bucharest material next.

What was the Bucharest material? What was the kernel of it?

I can't answer that because the kernel for me is always just a different group of people in a different setting. And in Bucharest, we were in a cultural center that had lots of big soft chairs and conference tables. There's a mythical character that has surfaced in some of my movies. People are always talking about "David Williamson." David Williamson this, David Williamson that. I forget if we were talking about David Williamson in Bucharest or the other character whose been surfacing, Rainer Thompson. I know that when I go to work on the material from Buffalo, which we also had a very interesting space, the title of that is going to be: *My Name is Rainer Thompson and I Have Lost It Completely* [later re-titled *Once Every Day*]. I'm not sure what the Bucharest material is called.

Who are these two characters? They are just made up?

They are archetypal. You know, names like that have a resonance, as I assume certain character names had for W. C. Fields. For "David Williamson" I wanted the most banal American name I could think of, and there's one American character in one of my favorite novels, this 1,500-page novel by Heimito von Doderer, a Viennese novelist, named somebody Williams, and I was thinking of that.

"Rainer Thompson," sounds Austrian to me, the end of high cultural empire, which is sort of what that novel is about.

That's sort of what my work is about: the end of the high culture empire of Western Europe, which is no more. I've always been infatuated with it. I love Vienna. One of the great sadnesses of my life is that our filming organization went to Vienna but I got sick and I couldn't go.

I've always been ambivalent about America and American culture. For fifteen years of my life I was totally infatuated with France, and then with other European cultures. But it is sort of over.

Can you tell us about the most important mystical experience you have had and how it has influenced your theater?

I was in my early twenties. I had a moment that started out like an average neurotic episode. I was trying to get my wife at the time's attention and she keep saying, "Just a minute," and after this dragged out for a while I said, "OK, just forget it." And I threw myself head-first down onto the bed. And as I hit the bed, my whole head opened up. All of a sudden my head seemed to be a globe. It must have been six feet in diameter or possibly twenty feet in diameter. Everything inside of me was projected on the inside surface of the globe and everything on the outside was projected on the outside surface of the globe. Everything in the whole world. And now, of course, it was like a golden transparency: the inside and the outside were on the same plane surrounding my head. Everything was perfect. This was accompanied by a feeling that everything for all time was there, and it was the way it should be. I didn't have to do anything, I had no more obligation, and the world was as it should be. That experience lasted for quite a while, at full intensity maybe ten minutes, then it faded. And as it faded I could still remember the feeling. I went to sleep and when I woke up in the morning I could remember the mechanics of the experience of the globe and everything else but I could no longer feel it.

Something similar happened a few days later. I was walking down Broadway, going to the store. As I stepped off the curb to cross the street, I turned my head slightly and I had a very strong feeling that a ray of light was hitting me from the sky. It wasn't nearly as intense as what happened to me the night before, but it seemed like a similar moment to the kind of illumination and I felt very good about that light in me.

I should add that during the same period I was waking up every night—and I'm not exaggerating—at least four times a night, screaming in the midst of terrible nightmares. And I woke the people living in the apartment above because I could hear them moving around. The dream always involved either somebody coming into the room or me rounding a corner, and there was somebody just staring at me with these huge, intense eyes. And I was paralyzed. I don't know what I was afraid of. It was significant that this kind of mystical experience was happening at the same time.

Back through the years, I've thought about these experiences but I didn't really know how to put them into my plays. I made reference to them in two plays with somebody talking about the experience, but I never succeeded really in integrating it. Though it has always been a feature of my plays that people stare at the audience, especially in the early days. The play was all about something being said to happen or the actors saying something and all the time glaring straight into the audience as if to say, "What are you going to do with this experience?"

And I relate that to the nightmare dreams. I have never abandoned this completely. The whole time I was making theater I always thought that what I was doing was in one way or another making things happen in general, and then trying to erase things that were happening by adding music or by adding lights in the eyes. I had different techniques that would erase the normal narrative of empathetic identification. And I think that can be related somehow to the feeling of being plopped on the bed—that the real world vanishes and what you're left with is the image of this real world, this timeless image in which everything is perfect.

In making film as opposed to theater, I'm no longer trying to arrange things, move people around and make things happen. As I've said many times, it's about watching. I've just realized today that I was setting up these tableaus (where the actors are arranged in some sort of echo of a particular painting, generally not a very famous painting, and then I manipulate the image in various ways) to capture a kind of fossil, a kind of residue that is left over from real experiences that these tableaus evoke.

And then by manipulating it electronically or with editing, I am erasing the reality of these fossils so that some other energy can enter, a wind from the cosmos. I named my theater "Ontological-Hysteric" because I was dealing with hysterical syndromes from nineteenth century Boulevard theater. Now what I am doing in film can't be called hysteric. The ontological something-or-other, maybe, but instead of psychological interaction of a hysteric nature, the films are dealing with the fossil remains that are evoked by images captured from generally non-major works of twentieth century art.

FILM NOTES

WHAT FOLLOWS IS NOT TO BE READ STRAIGHT THROUGH. PERHAPS NOT TO BE "READ" EXACTLY—BUT OCCASIONALLY "DIPPED INTO" WHEN ONE (MYSELF) FEELS BLOCKED AND EMPTY: BRIEF ENCOUNTERS TO RE-FRAME THAT EMPTINESS AS A MEANS TO . . .

**The pose
that internalizes**
(future, unexpected)

fingers
hands

You got distracted, and forgot (went a little dead)

TO OPERATE OUT OF NOTHING

TO MAKE IT ABOUT NOTHING

**IS TO DISCOVER A NEW WORLD
OF EVERYTHING**

Make the present THIN by seeing all connections
(ways to manipulate it, as a surface)

Or just

MAKE IT THIN (DARE THIS!)
   (wars with)

   (this is my inner contradiction)

A thin, blunt, brutal, naked present
   (this counterpoint, tension)

i.e. Duras—every word equal, don't allow caption pts. SO Hard to
have the necessary trust in the non-inflected

Intensify present

Plus

Intensify web-nature

   Entrance?
   Waiting?
Notice how I add points to re-glue attention

      —and THAT DISGUISES THE
      AWARENESS OF ON-GOING CRINKLING

SEE WORLD THIN OUT & SOMETHING

CRINKLES
TORN: between turning into a thing film
And the thing—RAW

With this mechanism, intensify relation
To the THINNESS of the PRESENT
And not to other mechanisms operating

Most film advertises what's happening
I detach from, and
Let something else bleed, crinkle

Eroticism of pose

Thin: to connect to orgasm—i.e., void, crack open
Every morsel shot thru with death
Wormholes of death (tunnel thru)

We see death as a big event, really, it's a tiny thing, the
System of death wormholes syncing up, it's at work ALL the time.
In the desired world
Everything breaks down to crystals

My "globe" experience, see "real" world as so thin

The world re-seen
As thin
& something
crinkles behind

Art is noticing things

+
How do I USE this mechanism (brain-art machine)

Rhythm-phrase (pause) repeat (music samples, phone tone, etc.)

IMPORTANT:
Take non-desirable images and weave
Them into web of truth!

It's all "self remembering" thru given tableau

The tableau (THE MOMENT) is the powerhouse
How do I use this mechanism

HOW DO I USE THIS MECHANISM
(old me, what's really happening here. . .)

Syncopate/asynchronic

WHAT'S REALLY GOING ON?

Not the present, past or future
But the RE-ITERATED "not being"
"my death"
not "possible"
yet is the impossible source/center of art
No death=no art, only entertainment

No director function (the machine
Films anything) only an editor function
& "molding, mutating" function

Theater/film give "memory" experiences usually: false fullness
* What's going on are re-iterated moments of absence * to be
    awake is to live in the elusive absence
un-readable density—12 tone
not you can't follow, but you can't HIERARCHIZE
    attack your own work is the work

Libido not pleasure-seeking

But object-seeking
(confront audience—what do you do with this?)

Confront objects—WHAT DO YOU DO with THIS?

Anything syncopated works

Do thing—stop—continue

Or

Do nothing: something passes—look== then back

To camera

It's not possible to show the reality behind the reality

Yet this is the important thing

SO ONE MUST SHOW THE NOT-SHOWING
(Of what can't be shown)

SYNCOPATE

　　1)　Span: choose the next word that forces the mind to
STRETCH to (re-direct)
(Monk at last minute hits different note)

　　2)　Single (univocal) substance, bifurcation into the multiple.

Change is significant when slight, and unimportant when massive

It's always <u>within</u> the inescapable given that small moves of freedom can occur

There is a film fighting to come out

MAKE IT LIKE STARCHED SHEETS

Flapping in the wind

When I edit:
The placement and balancing of mutual things to avoid closure
(syncopate)

to make a system in suspension over the issues of what life IS
finally

———

MONK reaching toward keys,
not chosen, to make, next one most necessary

I SHRED my art
and that
is the subject, that shredding

art is evil
and work is to destroy it
(Levinas, Picard, Parmenides)
yet I end up with

Hard in film to get to the shredding point, use
lots of "blank"

Use "false"
the false rule
the false dead

NEVER AMPLIFY

FILM / STAGE

**different worlds, resonate between, NOT
AMPLIFICATION
of each other
(a second world is always going on elsewhere
—this is the subject)(this is the message)**

**Since life is ALWAYS in danger of solidifying into icon (Levinas)
or fixed scheme, perspective
art is the epitome of this
make art fight this
shred its tendency to "amplify"**

**Try to return to source,
which is NOT the thing presented
not the "fact" or subject**

NEVER FULFILL

NEVER DELIVER

ZENO!
Movement-stillness
one undercuts the other

1) film that makes you unable to think it

2) never to empathize with someone
but
introduced to what you do not understand
to THAT
will be a kernel of alertness in you
in your life geography
you will orbit it (like the God you don't understand)

3) bad art works to make you forget it's not embedded in the
panorama of life
good—
instead, break thru the item to . . . some hidden internal network

4) Make art, not for "YOU," but for a space waiting to receive it

5) Words
condensed
until everything is included
(the alternatives, the opposites)

6) Blank look, at the beloved

7) Have a non-crystalizable idea
that you nevertheless cramp on
Bad art cramps you on objects that are defined, and being so
eliminate all other objects

Only if film
is only a hint
if it denies the easy gratification
of image and story.

Otherwise there is
no CLAMP onto that
texture within which
is embedded—truth?
    (like gold is embedded in earth)
    (like God is . . .)

Film at best
makes you clamp with
expectation
of relieving the
tension
of "what will happen"

but what I want is
the clamp of
"IF" I empty myself of
NORMAL DISTRACTION
AND EXPECTATION—

it—(something)
will reveal itself

1) seeing using donut vision

**2) You are looking and being looked at
Make film so the look in the GAZE
of the one looked at
who looks at YOU**

3) In life—look
in art—be looked at
      and capture (record) that
      by looking at
      being the world

4) The face is a screen on which
you see a thing which
penetrates you
      leaving a "hole"
      with which you "see"
      the tableau through which
      I am photo-graphed

5) Capture objects prior to the symbolic

6) Gaze= knowledge of the "real"
      (seeing= symbolic 'reading')

7) "You look at me from a place
      I do not see:
      What place? (the real?)"

8) Not what object says, what it presents

9) It doesn't produce meaning
BUT DESIGNATES AN IMPOSSIBLE TO SEE

10) A scene in which
each point is identical with the others
(yet at the same time different)
All points as good as each other

---

art, to impart sensation of things as seen, not as KNOWN

such de-familiarization, immediately becomes—it's momentary! Don't hold it!

you can't stay in present, so keep returning to it
THIS IS MY FILM

people rely on peaks and valleys, shifts. Get over that!
rather STAY ALERT and watch for sudden shifts

YOU
CAN'T STAY
IN THE PRESENT
SO
KEEP
RETURNING TO IT

RETURNING TO IT
IS MY STYLE!

The subject is always
YOU WATCHING IT BEING WATCHED

(old) Film
Take moment & turn it into story link
Stories—we need—drug us
Turn life into "tellable"

BUT I
Want moments that
Suck us OUT of false
Story form
That leaves keys to another way
Of seeing, which transforms
World into emptiness

Emptiness also—is a cocoon, perhaps.
But in it
We enter our own emptiness, which
Touches—eternity

---

looking into no future

looking into no past—
The genius of the moment
is to let slip into nothingness
even the most intense longing or
reminiscence
—serving no purpose but
to articulate the here and now plus
every one of its deep
potent
connections

Everything circles back
On itself
Which is
   (fade in whisper)
OK by me . . .

I no longer want to
Show my art.

Make art to function
Like an icon
(it looks at you)

WHAT
SHALL
FOR ME REPLACE
MAKING THE OBJECT

    (WAIT for the answer)
       (Seeing and hearing)

    (QUESTIONING)

**NORMAL FILM, to make you forget your own power & freedom
This restores it in you—**

There is a need here
for the one who observes
this seemingly impenetrable configuration . . .
—and the location of the one who observes is
totally elsewhere
in that esoteric space
which is your space only
—your space

My task is to make something
Without a story,
That keeps offering CHANCES
To re-awaken
And "see"—into the
Full emptiness
Of each moment

my HUNGER
is to believe in a SOLID TIME UNIT
(eternity infinity)

It's all about editing things: in-out
shorten, repeat, gaps
select moments, atoms
TO SHAPE a NEW BEING in world
that doesn't flow in normal time-line
but is JUMPING from time-slice
to time-slice

Since I love having to make
small changes= to start looking
at film, make a small change in myself

Strong thought is circular
it starts and ends
in the same place,
but in making that circle
it encloses the whole

Thinking that
goes from
"here to there"
(narrative)
leaves out
"everything"

Systems between words
How is this read?
How is this constituted?

Truth—spoken continually but not heard.
Right now, spoken

Hidden, behind
What can be seen—
It's spoken

Remember—the INFLECTION
Is the speaking

The slight pause, that is
In fact—punctuation,
Is the speaking

i.e., **the punctuation is the speaking**

We are traveling slowly
Around the singular object
(the whole)
that never changes

————————

    (use different intros,
    and repeat)   (ah, OK, etc.)

"It does not change"
The one object that does not change

Slowly, it does not change

————————————

If it does not change
    (you don't see it because it does
    not change, but it does not change)
one no longer sees it.
But it does not change

Surf   burrow

                                    Mole
                                    Drill

Create   traveler
(city, farm   nomad
domesticate   "journey"

"Ivan terrible" with Rabinovitch
new energy—non-Mickey Mouse
allows one to see Barthian "extra"

so

Hold image
And let extra RAYS
FLY OFF
(the concrete "silver cords")

all reflects all
(attached with)
World is chattering behind images
That "intend"
(to giggle at intention)
consciousness intends—
but if it didn't?

I.E. invisibilize.
See divine (daimon) in self
Burning in transformation
Come and go

WAIT FOR DIVINE IN SELF TO
EMERGE, in or between
Make adjustments
To assist that

We are
Beyond what we are

Watch for the beyond
What each one is
That is invisible
In each one

Go straight to
What you fear

Boredom
Death
NOTHING HAPPENS

"we live in a ruthless universe"
         (no entry into delightful activity)
there is great beauty (Tintoretto) and
absolutely no guarantees (Stasis! No
enter the flow)
Everything masquerading as its
         Opposite (stasis)
Love traps the soul (dance)
Strife sets it free (strife= rigor
         mortise : when strife comes, you are
         PARALYZED. Can't dance)

ANTI-DANCE
Trust in strife, paralysis
Not in dancing

Gurdjieff self-remember is METIS
Theater= (art)=
Not be carried away (as in life)
But SAVOR

Bypass the mind
But not emotion
But thinking in breath (eye-
De-focus!)

Deception is everything
Hold stasis, don't you then see it?
Hold still, look at a "tradition" (thinking
Or psychology)
Breathe as you look at it

Perceive all things turn **invisible**
DISSOLVING

Dismemberment from stasis

But add everything (grafts, i.e.,
Garbage) not to evoke whole world
But (food) to grow something else

You must grow the world
(actors, I return you to your
real self)

Important—find a way to
Make it hang together
Even when it is only—
        (isolated images—)
        (a data base)
        yet "build" them into
        a whole and formal
        "ritual" preparation form
for something like i.e. Passover—
leave a place for angel
or: decorate for a festive
        (what I do with shots)
_____
Art that "expresses" always falls short
(people with arms/tree branches)
It convinces about the mood, or re-enforces meaning
But that makes it go plastically dead
And stop vibrating like life, becomes a "sign" that no
        Longer holds secrets
Rather than express CONTRADICT
Just like life does (why it vibrates)
_____

Break up words
Pause: between words
WITHIN WORDS

_____

To KEEP ONE FROM
FALLING BACK INTO THINKING

It's rare, something gets out of chain
Of cause-effect, to FULLY APPEAR.
Pure events. True strangeness which
Alone fascinates. Can't be "interpreted"
Or deciphered

Get to that stage where you
Wipe out thought

An event, a being, a word—resolves
All efforts at explanation
No longer of causal order
(like speed: intense but dispassionate)

The event, as it emerges, before
It's "interpreted" into the system.
That moment—that flash
HOW TO SUSTAIN IT !

Never—commit to a single
Level of reality. Something else is
Always going on—disrupting
Your engagement (in happiness
Suffering, passion, etc.)

Tune to more accurate rendering
Of the human state, manifest as a
Being who belongs neither to the
World of social/psychological reality
Nor to world of his spiritual longing
But uncomfortably suspended in the
Tension between those 2 levels.

That state of tension, in which one falls
Towards one realm, only to be

Immediately pulled back toward the
other, only to fall short & fall back, the
pulled, then falls back

Art, seduces one, attracts one
To another world THEN YOU
REALIZE that is a prison, and it
Must be destroyed, create a rift
——Not a film, not a play
BUT notes for a film: or a play

Film= opportunity to LAY IN
SOUND against "whatever it is"

DON'T MAKE IT BETTER, JUST
INSIST IT IS WHAT IT IS

Image destroyed by word,
Destroyed by sound, destroyed by
Silence,

Saturate with SENSATION?
CRACK THE KERNEL of work,
Image, sound—what's in the
Fissure that covers all things
                    Not navigation
Of those "dummies" standing in
for— (Constructions propped up
by convention, etc.: BUT the empty
fullness that saturates—

NOT WHERE IT GOES
BUT HOW IT DEEPENS
WHERE IT IS

Ontology of the PRESENT
Deepen the present

UNFOLD THE PRESENT

"almost nothing" instant. "Peak"
(and LIVE in that peak—impossible?)
where being ceases to be something
and nothing ceases to be "nothing."
Explosive atom,

UNFOLD (Crystallization of)
THE PRESENT.

Art not as act of saying, but DOING.
DOING things with words.
Making is different from saying

Reveal while effacing (affirm
While denying)

Great things (crucial things) are
eternally pending, and never
manifest themselves

Strike a (tension) pose
: waiting for ecstasy-
revelation (adjust)

neither speak nor be
silent—give signs.

Creative acts (ecstasy)
Are discontinuous.

(singing does away with
saying—quiets chatter.
Posing is quieting
"chatter" of action.

EXTRACT parts of phrases
Re-combine
Things laid against things

To generate source material (hard):
to re-combine (delight)

Don't "deliver" a fulfilled idea, item,
but only hover, suspended.
    ("breakfast pose" Breathe heavily,
    on the verge: of being SEIZED from
    THE INSIDE)

Suspend coming to arrived sense, so
All hovers

Not about capturing the feel of
"real life" (artificial pretense &
prison) in which people are buffeted
by the (inner and outer) world they are
hypnotized by.
        But rather construct a
"staging area," where one lets death
enter (as one "dies" to the "effective"
participation in the living-death of the
life-illusion)
and one, in that
    STAGING AREA, from which
Involvement has been drained, from which
"effective manipulation" is banished—
one opens to the inevitable tree that
DEATH SEEDS. THE STAGING AREA—
Simply wait.

Descend into the hibernating state of
withdrawal from engagement,
and a garden grows.
Ripe—fruit—DAZZLES

Create each scene: a staging area
In which to incubate
                Where I can withdraw
Into that arena where I can connect
With what—underlies (darkness!)
Where death is no longer, (by twisting us
Into the masked version of ourself which
Functions like puppets—)
TAKING TAKING TAKING.
But death is FROZEN beside us—suspended
As we are.
Partners

All you have is the NOW, this
Moment of consciousness.
Trap, is to fall into time (death.
Action in the world)
All theater (discussion, nature,
writing, filming to "involve")
pulls us into "time"—which is
death. I.e.—living death.

Things FALL into existence, the
Universe FALLS into existence
"gravity" is original sin.
To SPIN is to transcend (existence)
Which is why planets, atoms, spin.
WORDS should also spin, (pivot)
One should internally, spin.
****

Innumerable procedural methods
Hovering, waiting for items to act
Upon:
Exercise these methods in (limbo)
Make a kind of music amidst them-
Selves?
Try out a variety of procedural
Methods—but to release their radiance,
Apply them in an arena wherein that
Radiance will not be dampened by
The sudden (unfortunate) gravity of
The hypnotic world (come to under-
Stand gravity as original sin).

All the above is KNOWN: what is the
OUTSIDE THE KNOWN?

MAKE SOMETHING
COME INTO THIS WORLD
THAT IS NOT IN THIS
WORLD

_____

Direct Confrontation
"What do you do with
this" Make the JUMP
through this locked door!
(Not "come thru this
inviting open door . . .")

Looking up references
Digging to know
Dig dig
(the lost object)
this is what I do

the secret of life
(the lost object)
is to be found
hidden inside death

Never let it settle
Into some "real"
Identifiable, gratifying
 "thing" (you "relax" into)
NO! Never sink into
The desired effect or
"reality"
ATTACK-ERASE its
"affect"
so stripped flesh, down
to a "potential"

Technique to make
One focus on
Present of the world
As a THING
Presented
To consciousness
(not to get
lost again in the
world—which leads
no-where (no escape)

Restaurant in Zurich
Inviting
But stop: go no further
To go further is to
See your own SELF
PROJECTED
But stop
The world
Is "other" than
What it is
If it is inviting
It is to trick you)

Dissolve: this tableau
Picture—duck-rabbit
World you know, no longer
CAN SWITCH
New world, still
PALPITATES with
Potential
Switch or dissolve

In making an experience
Stronger, that destroys the
Complexity and multi-level
Harmony and tension
Between parts

I.E., change the world vs. do
Something COMPLEX that has
no effect on anybody

Use tools of theater to make
music

Words not to explain, but
To re-tune

Never complete a thought
(sentence) which is to
fall into . . .

The desire to perform
Certain behaviors
(a syntax) life never allows
& so build a new world out
of "non-utilitarian" moves.

WITHDRAWAL IS EVERYTHING!
Withdraw help (explanation,
Story, idea even)
THIS PROVOKES THE
Sleeping self to . . .

---

1) Here, where I am not

2) Write "NET" not a solid.

3) Old—write intentioness at work, vs. now—write absence, mind is elsewhere

4) Old—given object to contemplate. Now—give object removal, HOLE where object was.

5) Something in me is not me

6) (Forgetting names: "You are not David Williamson, so I need not remember that your name is David Williamson"

7) Catch it with a cloth, pattern on cloth, but work to open hole (the weave) so "IT" shines thru (vs. most, cloth fixed to "shape" echoing pattern on thrown cloth)

8) "What's REALLY going on here?" (Names are forgotten) Free things from their names

9) Condense in a single (silly) moment, the weight of an entire life (a whole universe)

10) At each moment, stage (film) GAP between sensible and intelligible

11) Stare at audience. You are being played: here where I am not— Not by me

12) What is ineffable demands to remain so: make a cage for it

13) Remember: to desire is to be fulfilled. To achieve is to be imprisoned we lack creation: We lack resistance to the present

---

I make art, so that there is an OCCASION in which
All the dreck that does involuntarily arise in consciousness

Can be—made transparent: so—ground of being shows thru:
So point is not to make a THING: but to let something "show thru"
On the verge (it can never BE there, remember)

Plays to re-focus (de-focus?) the mental mechanism
Why? To connect, as a different kind of consciousness
comes into play—with a different world, which is
Indeed available to us, not this one where people navigate to have
power over others, which en-meshes one in time, but one
In which the de-focusing itself, offers us, freedom (released into
eternal instants)

Normally, live in
A world built of habit
And illusion:
Why not build a world out of FLASHES of truth
Break-thru
(it's about twisting something—anything, the less important the
better—) into the truth. It shines thru the CRACKS that
result from that twisting

messages imprison us
make a rhythm to re-frame what
we are force-fed, to make a
space of freedom FROM—
(so you can't connect the dots)
:my "have no effect"
You are FREE. I don't build a
New prison.
(NO to the present!)

turn away from "chatter" (whereas
most people want to get in the nest of chatter)

Monastery film, (objects, cuts) vs. the LOOK
At us. I.E. the LOOK that EMPTIES US (of chatter)
It doesn't "cut away" to new object.
It denies us the CUT-AWAY that

Re-enforces the idea the world is
Full of trinkets for you.

to move into the zone of which I am speaking . . . it is
necessary to realize the following.
There is a mother lode of dense material, burning
in black fire, and that mother lode is separated from us by
layers and layers of safety material called earth and
reality and human beings, and the task of some very few
of those human beings is to explore the intricate protective structures surrounding that dense mother lode, and to find,
just occasionally, a tiny rift, a tiny gap, in that protective layering,
through which one may then catch just a glimpse of rare black fire.

———————

yet : Things most "revelatory" (nuggets of un-canny) I can't stay
with. I need re-start, as if "No, you didn't get it, there will be no further Revelation, just another impasse (as "expectation" habit rises
in you)

Revelation will never come (Balthasar) we must LIVE in terms of
that
Built-in HUNGER which **CAN'T** be satisfied
(but AVOID substitution food!)
FRUSTRATION is key! (metaxy)

Go to strife? Metis.

**If I can say something that eludes exact
Conceptualization, only then can I remain truly alive—i.e.,
Freedom still.**

**WITHOUT LANGUAGE WE ARE VICTIMS OF THE
WORLD, PRISONERS OF THE WORLD**

**BUT LANGUAGE BUILDS A NEW, ALTERNATIVE
PRISON; UNLESS—USED IN A WAY**

**THAT KEEPS TRIPPING UP FIXED
CONCEPTUALIZATION
WITHOUT TAKING A FORM
THAT MAKES US
HUNGRY FOR CLARIFICATION;
AND STILL LETS US
SURF REALITY.**

A voice inside me says—

The self-evident lack of belief, leads, to no belief
On the basis of such a powerful experience

Forgetful of real things
Opportunity arises

I shall entertain of my flexible point of view
Only if I am able to access words not yet
Functional in my vocabulary

When the not yet is a full participant
Only then I shall be able to fully access
Past experience

The beginning, wastes the occasion
Of the opportunity
That never returns

The emptiness, of the inner world
Is a mistake, that fills
Every void

The only problem: how to sustain attention
When there is no story (or event)
—In the face of restlessness

stories exist to "stop" pain (restlessness of
too complex a world to make sense of)

Impatience cures its restlessness with a fixed
Gaze with enough "depth of field" to locate
A vanishing point and no more! (climax)
Bad: feelings underlined, links in chain building
Us: whole world implicated in each powerhouse
moment

_____

_____(Lacan)
truth only accessible thru half-saying, cannot be said completely
because beyond this half there is nothing to say

cannot say anything not a tautology (everything that can be said is
only nonsense:)

_____

If art "tells the truth" (haha) one can "argue" with it
If one "half-says" it infects one and one COMPLETES IT and gets to
know a bit more of oneself.

We start to speak, and language takes over. BLOCK THAT!

Realize that all you LUSTED after was a trick, and illusion

Silent, black seed of darkness—plant or graft THAT in you "split"
The waiting inside "not knowing"

CONFRONT that you no longer function

What does one do when one finds the world, as one ages, to be
transformed and diminished by vulgar interests and art.
The world previously accessed by one's lifelong beloved objects—
Now that one is in a "new world" one no longer has the patience to
immerse oneself in the objects of one's previous devotion (perhaps
even discovering one did not love those things, but rather the
"Aura" of their exuded life)
So one must be TRUE to that no-longer-functioning (inner world)
because to wholly adopt the new is to deny what one has become thru
years of struggle—stamping out all one's worthwhile accumulation.
So—one must simply HOVER on the cusp of death, and confront
again and again confront (vibrating between worlds) the paradox

that one's acquired mastery is now useless.
Truth is in this

Do not "DO"
(i.e., intend a play or film)
Receive material
THEN
Work it, make it reveal
(burn away)
the non-moving beneath

occult surfacing of sign; ON FIRE

TABLEAU: DEATH ENTERS
The not-you—can't identify with it—be twisted out of self-shape
        Or—it's just more you.

In details, make it awkwardly raw (even in whole shape)
Real: but not the inherited, efficient shape to show
        This move—twist it, deface it, dirty it
        (or in music choice, or sudden silence,
        over-exposure, light—"roughen it")
Yet the WHOLE GRID is orchestrated into elegant & Concise

Lifting: out of the on-going—   STOP!
THE MOMENT IS THE POWERHOUSE

Creativity as my myth

Response (art) to AWE (light of)
Un-sayable or in words

This frightening thing in fact brings happiness
Where are you between two thoughts?

What does it "mean"?
No—
It releases something—in you
(what meaning to a sunset)
Normal life doesn't RELEASE something in me that wants to
BLOSSOM

MY JOB is to make things (only)
Radiate
      (aesthetic arrest)

————————————————

You begin to grow in darkness (womb, etc.)
Enter the darkness
Closes eyes, (blindfold?)
and enter the light

"Let's improve the world" You don't marry someone to
improve them.
Present objects in such a way that they shine.
Things you looked at with indifference, will be radiant
Aesthetic arrest

Don't be impressed by
Discourse, which leads to
      Need for "climax," an end, a meaning
      I.e. distraction

Just present yourself
(Parmenides—entering death

PUBLICATION HISTORY

The manifestos were originally published in *Richard Foreman: Plays and Manifestos*, edited by Kate Davy (New York University Press, 1976), and first appeared in the following magazines:

"Ontological-Hysteric Manifesto I" in *Performance*, Vol. 1, No. 2 (April 1972).

"Ontological-Hysteric Manifesto II" in *The Drama Review: TDR*, Vol. 18, No. 3 (September 1974).

"Ontological-Hysteric Manifesto III" in *The Drama Review: TDR*, Vol. 19, No. 4 (December 1975).

The essays were originally published in *Reverberation Machines: The Later Plays and Essays* (Station Hill Press, 1985), and first appeared in the following magazines:

"How Truth . . . Leaps (Stumbles) Across Stage" in *Performing Arts Journal*, Vol. 5, No. 2 (Winter 1981).

"14 Things I Tell Myself when I fall into the trap of making the writing imitate 'experience'" in *Tel Quel*, No. 68 (Winter 1976).

"The Carrot and The Stick" in *October*, Vol. 1, No. 1 (Spring 1976).

"How to Write a Play" in *Performing Arts Journal*, Vol. 1, No. 2 (Autumn 1976).

"How I Write My (Plays: Self)" in *The Drama Review: TDR*, Vol. 21, No. 4 (December 1977).

The interview by Morgan von Prelle Pecelli was originally published on the website *Reality Sandwich* as "Seeing What's Really There: A Talk with Richard Foreman," http://www.realitysandwich.com/.

RICHARD FOREMAN is the founder and artistic director of the not-for-profit Ontological-Hysteric Theater in New York City (founded 1968). Foreman has written, directed and designed more than fifty of his own plays, both in New York City and abroad. He has received numerous awards and citations, including OBIE awards for Directing, Best Play, and Sustained Achievement; an Annual Literature Award from the American Academy of Arts and Letters; a Lifetime Achievement in the Theater Award from the National Endowment for the Arts; the PEN/Laura Pels Foundation Master American Dramatist Award; a MacArthur "Genius" Fellowship; the Edwin Booth Award for Theatrical Achievement; a Ford Foundation play development grant; a Rockefeller Foundation playwrights grant and a Guggenheim Fellowship for Playwriting. In 2004, he was elected Officer of the Order of Arts and Letters of France. Since the early 1970s, his work and company have been funded by the NEA and NYSCA, in addition to many other foundations and private individuals.

His archives and work materials were acquired by the Bobst Library at NYU in 2004.

The Ontological-Hysteric Theater was located in the historic St. Mark's Church-in-the-Bowery, in New York City's East Village neighborhood from 1992 to 2010, and served as a home to Foreman's annual productions as well as to other local and international artists. During these years Ontological began presenting emerging theater artists. The program, now known as the Incubator Arts Project, continues to produce and present at St. Mark's Church.

In the early 1980s a branch of the theater was established in Paris and funded by the French government.

Foreman's plays have been co-produced by such organizations as New York's Public Theater/New York Shakespeare Festival, La MaMa, The Wooster Group, the Festival d'automne in Paris and the Vienna Festival. He has collaborated (as librettist and stage director) with composer Stanley Silverman on eight music-theater pieces produced by the Music-Theater Group and the New York City Opera. He wrote and directed the opera *What to Wear* (music by Michael Gordon), which was produced in 2006 at CalArts's REDCAT Theatre in Los Angeles. He has also directed and designed many productions with major theaters around the world, including *The Threepenny Opera*, *The Golem* and plays by Václav Havel, Botho Strauss and Suzan-Lori Parks for The Public Theater/New York Shakespeare Festival; *Die Fledermaus* for the Paris Opera; *Don Giovanni* for the Opera de Lille; Philip Glass's *Fall of the House of Usher* for American Repertory Theatre and the Maggio Musicale in Florence; *Woyzeck* at Hartford Stage; *Don Juan* at the Guthrie Theater and The Public Theater/New York Shakespeare Festival; Kathy Acker's *The Birth of the Poet* at the Brooklyn Academy of Music and the RO Theater in Rotterdam; and Gertrude Stein's *Doctor Faustus Lights the Lights* at the Autumn festivals in Berlin and Paris.

He wrote and directed his first feature film, *Strong Medicine*, in 1981. His latest feature film, *Once Every Day*, came out in 2013 and was featured in both the New York Film Festival and in the Berlin Film Festival.

He holds degrees from Brown University (BA, Magna Cum Laude, Phi Beta Kappa) 1959; Yale School of Drama (MFA, Playwriting) 1962; and an Honorary Doctorate from Brown University, 1993. He was born in New York City on June 10, 1937.

There are numerous collections of Foreman's plays, and books that study his work. Works by Foreman include: *Plays with Films* (Contra Mundum Press, 2013); *Bad Boy Nietzsche! and Other Plays* (TCG, 2007); *Paradise Hotel and Other Plays* (The Overlook Press, 2001); *No-Body: A Novel in Parts* (The Overlook Press, 1996); *My Head Was a Sledgehammer: Six Plays* (The Overlook Press, 1995); *Unbalancing Acts: Foundations for a Theater* (Pantheon Books, 1992; TCG, 1994); *Love & Science: Selected Music-Theatre Texts* (TCG, 1991); *Reverberation Machines: The Later Plays and Essays* (Station Hill Press, 1985); and *Richard Foreman: Plays and Manifestos* (New York University Press, 1976).

Books that devote their entirety or a chapter to Richard Foreman and his work include: *ABCDery of Richard Foreman*, Anne Berevolitch (Editions du Sud, Paris, 1999); *Die Bühne als Szene Denkens*, Markus Wessendorf (Alexander Verlag, Berlin, 1998); *Directors in Rehearsal: A Hidden World*, Susan Letzler Cole (Routledge, 1992); *The Director's Voice: Twenty-One Interviews*, Arthur Bartow (TCG, 1988); *In Their Own Words: Contemporary American Playwrights*, David Savran (TCG, 1988); *The Other American Drama*, Marc Robinson (The Johns Hopkins University Press, 1994); *Postmodernism and Performance*, Nick Kaye (Macmillan, 1994); *Richard Foreman*, edited by Gerald

Rabkin (PAF Books: Art + Performance/The Johns Hopkins University Press. 1999); *Richard Foreman and the Ontological-Hysteric Theater,* Kate Davy (UMI Research Press, 1981); *Theater at the Margins: Texts for a Post-Structured Stage,* Erik MacDonald (University of Michigan Press, 1993); and *Tradizione e Ricerca,* Franco Quadri (Giulio Einaudi, Editore, 1982).